- Go to **awmi.net/sg435** to download PDFs of the following resources for each lesson in this study guide:
  - ○ Outlines
  - ○ Discipleship Questions
  - ○ Scriptures

- Share as many copies as you'd like.

- These documents are not for resale.

HOW TO FIND GOD'S WILL

PART 1 OF 3

STUDY GUIDE

Unless otherwise indicated, all Scripture quotations are taken from the *King James Version* of the Bible.

THE HOLY BIBLE, NEW INTERNATIONAL VERSION®, NIV® Copyright © 1973, 1978, 1984, 2011 by Biblica, Inc.™ Used by permission. All rights reserved worldwide.

The author has emphasized some words in Scripture quotations with underline.

How to Find God's Will Study Guide
ISBN: 978-1-59548-160-3

Copyright © 2013 by Andrew Wommack Ministries Inc.
PO Box 3333
Colorado Springs CO 80934-3333

awmi.net

TABLE OF CONTENTS

HOW TO USE YOUR STUDY GUIDE

HOW TO USE YOUR STUDY GUIDE

Whether you are teaching a class, leading a small group, discipling an individual, or studying on your own, this study guide is designed for you! Here's how it works:

Each study consists of a **Lesson, Outline, Teacher's Guide, Discipleship Questions, Answer Key**, and **Scriptures**—all of which have been divided into sections. Within the study, each section is a continuation of the previous section.

Outline for Group Study:
  I. If possible, briefly review the previous study by going over the **Answer Key/Teacher's Guide** answers for the **Discipleship Questions/Teacher's Guide** questions.
  II. Read the current section for the **Lesson** or **Teacher's Guide** aloud (e.g., 1.1, 1.2).
      A. Be sure that each student has a copy of the **Outline**.
      B. While the **Lesson** section or **Teacher's Guide** section is being read, students should use their **Outlines** to follow along.
  III. Once the **Lesson** section or **Teacher's Guide** section is read, facilitate discussion and study using the **Discipleship Questions/Teacher's Guide** questions (the questions are all the same).
      A. Read aloud one question at a time.
      B. The group should use their **Outlines** to assist them in answering the questions.
      C. Have them read aloud each specifically mentioned scripture before answering the question.
      D. Discuss the answer/point from the **Lesson**, as desired.
      E. As much as possible, keep the discussion centered on the scriptures and the **Lesson** section or **Teacher's Guide** section points at hand.
      F. Remember, the goal is understanding (Matt. 13:19).
      G. One individual should not dominate the discussion, but try to draw out the quieter ones for the group conversation.
      H. Repeat the process until all of the questions are discussed/answered.

Materials Needed:
  Study guide, Bible, and enough copies of the **Outline, Discipleship Questions**, and **Scriptures** for each student. (PDFs of the **Outlines, Discipleship Questions**, and **Scriptures** can be downloaded via the URL located on the first page of this study guide.)

Outline for Personal Study:
  I. Read the current **Lesson** section or **Teacher's Guide** section.
      A. Read additional information, if provided.
      B. Meditate on the given scriptures, as desired.
  II. Answer the corresponding **Discipleship Questions/Teacher's Guide** questions.
  III. Check your work with the **Answer Key/Teacher's Guide** answers.

Materials Needed:
  Study guide, Bible, and a writing utensil.

GOD CREATED YOU
FOR A PURPOSE

LESSON 1.1

Recently I was teaching at a Bible college about God's will and asked the question, "How many of you aren't sure you're doing what God created you for?" I said, "You may want it, you may desire it, you may be praying that God will take all of the things you do and use them to further His kingdom, but how many of you aren't certain you're doing what God created you to do?" Over half of the people in the room raised their hands to say they weren't positive they were doing what God called them to do—and those were fanatics who came out on a Thursday morning just to hear the Gospel!

You are not going to accidentally fulfill God's will. It doesn't happen unintentionally or by coincidence. Seeing God's will realized in your life means, first of all, finding out what unique purpose He created you for. In nature, water always seeks the path of least resistance, and human nature does the same thing if you allow it to. You can end up meandering through life, allowing obstacles you encounter to determine what direction you go in. But it doesn't have to be that way. God intends for you to experience the satisfaction of a life well lived. You can do this if you are willing to do more than just go with the flow—even a dead fish can float downstream.

Accomplishing the things we were created to achieve means making a deliberate effort to find, follow, and fulfill God's will. When I put forth effort to discover my God-given purpose, it was a critical turning point in my life. I was in high school at the time, and until then, everything had been decided for me. But as I approached the end of my senior year, I realized I was going to have to start making some decisions on my own. This brought me face to face with the question we all eventually ask: "What is the purpose for my life?"

One thing I am grateful that I learned while growing up in church is that God created everyone with a purpose. Your parents may not have known you were coming, but God did. God created you. You didn't evolve. You aren't a mistake. God created you, and He created you for a reason.

As I wrestled with what to do about my future, I knew that God had a purpose for my life. So, I didn't want to just randomly pick a direction. I began asking people in my church, "How do you know God's will for your life? How do you find it?" Unfortunately, nobody could tell me. I didn't know of any method for discovering God's will, so I started studying the Word of God. I knew that the Bible contained knowledge about God, so I figured it was a good place to look for God's will for my life. I began to stay up until two or three o'clock every morning studying the Bible.

I had read the Bible every day of my life since I was a little kid, but I never really studied it. So, I went out and bought a Bible commentary to help me understand everything. I had about five volumes of these big old heavy books, and I would sit there and study every single verse. I remember using a lamp with a flexible gooseneck that allowed me to position it in different ways. I used to pull the lamp down over my Bible and read with my head perched above the lamp casing. Whenever I started to fall asleep, my forehead would nod down onto the lamp, and it would burn me—jarring me back awake so I would keep on reading. That was how I forced myself to stay up and read the Bible.

Although I read through the entire Bible two or three times that year, I didn't feel like God had shown me anything special. I didn't receive any specific revelations. I was just preparing the ground. Before planting a seed, you have to dig out the rocks and prepare the ground so the seed can sink in. That's what I was doing—I was seeking the Lord. I did that for over a year, and then, all of a sudden, something opened up.

> *I beseech you therefore, brethren, by the mercies of God, that ye present your bodies a living sacrifice, holy, acceptable unto God, which is your reasonable service. [2] And be not conformed to this world: but be ye transformed by the renewing of your mind, that ye may prove what is that good, and acceptable, and perfect, will of God.*
>
> ROMANS 12:1-2

This passage of Scripture came alive to me. It burned in my heart. I spent months reading it and asking God, "What does this mean? How do I do it?" Then, some time later, I had a miraculous encounter with the Lord and experienced His love for me. It turned my life upside down, and for more than four months, I was caught up in the presence of God. It changed me.

Often when I talk about this miraculous encounter with God, people think it was a fluke—like lightning or something. They think, *You never know where it's going to strike.* Actually, I've heard that lightning doesn't come from the sky down. It looks that way, but there is a negative charge in the ground that attracts the lightning—so it really starts *in* the ground. You can see this in time-lapse photos of a lightning strike. The reality is that lightning strikes certain places for a reason.

Likewise, there are reasons that God, all of a sudden, captures one person's life with a miraculous encounter, while others don't encounter Him at all. It's true that you can't make God reveal something to you by saying, "God, tell me what I want to know, *right now.*" It doesn't work like that. But you *can* prepare your heart.

In my situation, I didn't really understand what was happening in me. I wasn't mature enough to know what was going on—I was just hungry for God. I wanted to know God's purpose for my life. I had been seeking Him in the best way I knew how to for eighteen months. It wasn't an accident that God showed up. I knew He had a purpose for me, and my life was turned around when I became hungry to discover it. As a result of my hunger, God touched me. And I've never gotten over it. It changed my life!

A popular misconception in the church today is that God winds us up like dolls and then lets us go our own way, leaving us to figure life out on our own. *If I get in a bind*, the thinking goes, *I can call on God and* maybe *He'll help me.* This kind of philosophy leads people to do their own thing and then ask God to bless it—instead of seeking Him for direction from the beginning.

Since I found God's will for my life, I don't ever pray for God to bless what I'm doing. I don't even pray for the meetings I hold around the country—which shocks some people. I have been asked, "You didn't spend time praying and interceding before the meeting?" No, because God told me to hold those meetings. He would be unjust to command me to do something and then expect me to do it in my own strength and power. God gives me an anointing to do what He has called me to do. It's the same for everyone. When you are doing what God called you to do, you don't have to spend time asking for His blessing or praying for Him to move on your behalf. *God has already blessed what He told you to do.*

One reason so many people are praying for God to come to their assistance is because they aren't doing what He told them to do. Others may have stumbled into God's will for their lives, but they don't have that assurance and joy that comes from knowing they are exactly where He wants them to be.

Is Someone Waiting on You?

I believe there is a supernatural peace that goes along with being in the center of God's will. It does something in you when you know you are where God wants you to be. I remember an encounter I had in Charlotte, North Carolina, where I have ministered every year since the 1980s. A friend of mine has a business there and invites me to come speak to his employees. One year I spoke at his business, and as I was leaving, I saw an Asian woman answering the phones. I had never seen her before, so I stopped and started talking to her.

"Are you new here?" I asked.

"Yes," she said, "I just started last week."

"Oh, okay. Well, how come you weren't back there with the rest of the employees?"

"I'm the new person, so they had me answer the phone," she answered. "Who are you?"

I told her who I was, and she said, "What do you do?"

"I'm a minister."

"For who?" she asked.

"For Jesus." I said.

"You must be the one!" she exclaimed.

I asked her what she was talking about, and she explained that she was a Buddhist. The night before, she had been performing her Buddhist worship and was suddenly disillusioned with the whole thing and said, "This isn't it. Buddha is *not* it." She told me how she spoke out, "God, I know *You* are real. I know You exist, but I don't know *who* You are. Would you reveal Yourself to me?" Then she recounted how a pulsating ball of light appeared and hung right in front of her. She said she knew it was God, but she asked anyway, "Who are you?" A voice replied, "Tomorrow, I'll send you a man who will tell you who I am."

"You must be the one," she exclaimed again.

"I'm the one," I said.

I went on to tell her about Jesus, and she was born again and baptized in the Holy Spirit. It was awesome! I left that place thinking, *God, I was in the right place at the right time!* I was exactly where I was supposed to be. God knew He could count on me to be there and to follow His leading, so He told that woman to expect me. I can't even describe the peace, satisfaction, and joy that comes from knowing you are right where God wants you to be. If that doesn't make you have a good day, nothing will. Something happens when you know that with everything, you are doing what God created you to do.

Many people have never felt the satisfaction of knowing, beyond the shadow of a doubt, that they are doing what God made them for. No believer should live that way. God created you for something better than wandering aimlessly through life. You have a purpose.

I.   You are not going to accidentally fulfill God's will.

    A. Seeing God's will realized in your life means, first of all, finding out what unique purpose He created you for.

    B. You can end up meandering through life, allowing obstacles you encounter to determine what direction you go in, but it doesn't have to be that way.

    C. God intends for you to experience the satisfaction of a life well lived.

    D. You can do this if you are willing to do more than just go with the flow—even a dead fish can float downstream.

II. Accomplishing the things you were created to achieve means making a deliberate effort to find, follow, and fulfill God's will.

    A. When I put forth effort to discover my God-given purpose, it was a critical turning point in my life.

    B. I began asking people in my church "How do you find God's will for your life?" but nobody could tell me.

    C. I knew that the Bible contained knowledge about God, so I figured it was a good place to look for God's will for my life.

> *I beseech you therefore, brethren, by the mercies of God, that ye present your bodies a living sacrifice, holy, acceptable unto God, which is your reasonable service. [2] And be not conformed to this world: but be ye transformed by the renewing of your mind, that ye may prove what is that good, and acceptable, and perfect, will of God.*
>
> ROMANS 12:1-2

    D. I spent months reading this passage of Scripture and asking God, "What does this mean? How do I do it?"

    E. Then I had a miraculous encounter with the Lord and experienced His love for me.

    F. I wasn't mature enough to know what was going on, but I was hungry for God.

    G. It wasn't an accident that He showed up.

    H. I've never gotten over it—it changed my life!

III. A popular misconception in the church today is that God winds people up like dolls and then lets them go their own way, leaving them to figure life out on their own.

    A. This kind of philosophy leads people to do their own thing and then ask God to bless it—instead of seeking Him for direction from the beginning.

    B. Since I found God's will for my life, I don't ever pray for Him to bless what I'm doing.

C. God would be unjust to command me to do something and then expect me to do it in my own strength and power.

D. He gives me an anointing to do what He has called me to do, and it's the same for everyone.

E. *God has already blessed what He told you to do.*

F. One reason so many people are praying for God to come to their assistance is because they aren't doing what He told them to do.

G. Others may have stumbled into God's will for their lives, but they don't have that assurance and joy that comes from knowing they are exactly where He wants them to be.

IV. It does something in you when you know you are where God wants you to be.

A. Can God count on you to follow His leading?

B. Many people have never felt the satisfaction of knowing, beyond the shadow of a doubt, that they are doing what God made them for.

C. God created you for something better than wandering aimlessly through life.

D. You have a purpose.

1. You are not going to accidentally fulfill God's will. Seeing God's will realized in your life means, first of all, finding out what unique purpose He created you for. You can end up meandering through life, allowing obstacles you encounter to determine what direction you go in, but it doesn't have to be that way. God intends for you to experience the satisfaction of a life well lived. You can do this if you are willing to do more than just go with the flow—even a dead fish can float downstream.

1a.   Discussion question: Why do you think you can't accidentally fulfill God's will for your life?
Discussion question

1b.   What shouldn't determine the direction you go in?
A.   Obedience
B.   Obstacles
C.   Godly counsel
D.   All of the above
E.   None of the above
B.   Obstacles

1c.   What does God intend for you to experience?
The satisfaction of a life well lived

2. Accomplishing the things you were created to achieve means making a deliberate effort to find, follow, and fulfill God's will. When I put forth effort to discover my God-given purpose, it was a critical turning point in my life. I began asking people in my church "How do you find God's will for your life?" but nobody could tell me. I knew that the Bible contained knowledge about God, so I figured it was a good place to look for God's will for my life.

> *I beseech you therefore, brethren, by the mercies of God, that ye present your bodies a living sacrifice, holy, acceptable unto God, which is your reasonable service. [2] And be not conformed to this world: but be ye transformed by the renewing of your mind, that ye may prove what is that good, and acceptable, and perfect, will of God.*
>
> ROMANS 12:1-2

I spent months reading this passage of Scripture and asking God, "What does this mean? How do I do it?" Then I had a miraculous encounter with the Lord and experienced His love for me. I wasn't mature enough to know what was going on, but I was hungry for God. It wasn't an accident that He showed up. I've never gotten over it—it changed my life!

2a.   Accomplishing the things you were created to achieve means making a deliberate _____ to find, follow, and fulfill God's will.
   Effort

2b.   What was a critical turning point in Andrew's life?
   When he put forth effort to discover his God-given purpose

2c.   Discussion question: What does it tell you about Andrew's understanding of God that he went to the Bible to look for God's will for his life?
   Discussion question

2d.   When Andrew was hungry for God, what happened?
   A.   People discouraged it
   B.   He didn't care about anyone but himself
   C.   God showed up
   D.   He ordered a pizza
   E.   Nothing
   C.   God showed up

3. A popular misconception in the church today is that God winds people up like dolls and then lets them go their own way, leaving them to figure life out on their own. This kind of philosophy leads people to do their own thing and then ask God to bless it—instead of seeking Him for direction from the beginning. Since I found God's will for my life, I don't ever pray for Him to bless what I'm doing. God would be unjust to command me to do something and then expect me to do it in my own strength and power. He gives me an anointing to do what He has called me to do, and it's the same for everyone. *God has already blessed what He told you to do.* One reason so many people are praying for God to come to their assistance is because they aren't doing what He told them to do. Others may have stumbled into God's will for their lives, but they don't have that assurance, joy, and peace that comes from knowing they are exactly where He wants them to be.

3a.   The idea that God leaves you to figure life out on your own is what?
    A misconception

3b.   True or false: It's okay to do your own thing and ask God to bless it.
    False

3c.   Why don't you have to ask God to bless what He told you to do?
    Because He has already blessed it

3d.   What's one reason so many people are praying for God to come to their assistance?
    Because they aren't doing what He told them to do

3e.   Others may have stumbled into God's will for their lives, but what don't they have?
    That assurance, joy, and peace that comes from knowing they are exactly where He wants them to be

4. It does something in you when you know you are where God wants you to be. Can God count on you to follow His leading? Many people have never felt the satisfaction of knowing, beyond the shadow of a doubt, that they are doing what God made them for. God created you for something better than wandering aimlessly through life. You have a purpose.

4a.   Discussion question: Can God count on you to follow His leading? Why or why not?
    Discussion question

4b.   How well do you need to know that you are doing what God made you for?
    A. Beyond the shadow of a doubt
    B. Somewhat
    C. Not well at all
    D. All of the above
    E. None of the above
    A. Beyond the shadow of a doubt

4c.   Why isn't it good to wander aimlessly through life?
    Because you have a purpose

DISCIPLESHIP QUESTIONS • 1.1

1. Discussion question: Why do you think you can't accidentally fulfill God's will for your life?

_____

_____

_____

2. What shouldn't determine the direction you go in?
   A. Obedience
   B. Obstacles
   C. Godly counsel
   D. All of the above
   E. None of the above

3. What does God intend for you to experience?

_____

_____

_____

4. Accomplishing the things you were created to achieve means making a deliberate _____ to find, follow, and fulfill God's will.

5. What was a critical turning point in Andrew's life?

_____

_____

_____

6. Discussion question: What does it tell you about Andrew's understanding of God that he went to the Bible to look for God's will for his life?

_____

_____

_____

7. When Andrew was hungry for God, what happened?
   A. People discouraged it
   B. He didn't care about anyone but himself
   C. God showed up
   D. He ordered a pizza
   E. Nothing

8. The idea that God leaves you to figure life out on your own is what?

_____

_____

_____

9. True or false: It's okay to do your own thing and ask God to bless it.

10. Why don't you have to ask God to bless what He told you to do?

_____

_____

_____

11. What's one reason so many people are praying for God to come to their assistance?

_____

_____

_____

12. Others may have stumbled into God's will for their lives, but what don't they have?

_____

_____

_____

13. Discussion question: Can God count on you to follow His leading? Why or why not?

_____

_____

_____

14. How well do you need to know that you are doing what God made you for?
    A. Beyond the shadow of a doubt
    B. Somewhat
    C. Not well at all
    D. All of the above
    E. None of the above

15. Why isn't it good to wander aimlessly through life?

_____

_____

_____

ANSWER KEY • 1.1

1. *Discussion question*
2. B. Obstacles
3. The satisfaction of a life well lived
4. Effort
5. When he put forth effort to discover his God-given purpose
6. *Discussion question*
7. C. God showed up
8. A misconception
9. False
10. Because He has already blessed it
11. Because they aren't doing what He told them to do
12. That assurance, joy, and peace that comes from knowing they are exactly where He wants them to be
13. *Discussion question*
14. A. Beyond the shadow of a doubt
15. Because you have a purpose

ROMANS 12:1-2
I beseech you therefore, brethren, by the mercies of God, that ye present your bodies a living sacrifice, holy, acceptable unto God, which is your reasonable service. **[2]** And be not conformed to this world: but be ye transformed by the renewing of your mind, that ye may prove what is that good, and acceptable, and perfect, will of God.

LESSON 1.2

The only way to have perfect peace and joy is to point your life in the direction that God wants you to go. Otherwise, you may be praying to get rid of discouragement in your life when, in fact, the lack of peace you are experiencing is a result of not being in God's perfect will. When you aren't going in the right direction, He will sometimes turn you around by giving you a sense of unrest, or what I call a "holy dissatisfaction."

We need to understand that the holy dissatisfaction that comes from God is totally different from depression. The depression that comes from the world is a result of giving your attention to the flesh instead of focusing on the things of God (Rom. 8:6). The dissatisfaction that God uses to give direction to believers who are seeking Him is completely different from the turmoil of negative emotions. God doesn't use depression to guide us.

When my wife, Jamie, and I pastored a church in Seagoville, Texas, there were times that friends tried to talk us into leaving. They would say, "People aren't receiving the message, nobody wants you, just move on." It was true—people stayed away from our church by the droves. But we were committed to Seagoville. We loved the people and were happy, so we stayed there and kept on ministering.

Everything was great until one day when I was in church praying—it was like somebody flipped a switch on the inside of me. All of a sudden, I looked out the window, over the town, and thought, *God, what am I doing here? If this isn't the end of the world, you can see it from here.* The desires of my heart changed in an instant, and suddenly I *hated* being in Seagoville.

This change in how I felt was so abrupt that it kind of surprised me. It was only the day before that I was happy and excited about simply having the opportunity to minister there. Then, without any apparent reason, I didn't want to be in Seagoville anymore. I started praying and seeking God for clarity, and within an hour or two, I was convinced that God was telling me to leave. In fact, He even gave me a date. He told me that we would be leaving our house by the first of November. I was sure of it, so I started toward home wondering how I was going to tell Jamie that we were moving. When I arrived home, there was already a "For Sale" sign in our front yard!

I walked into the house and asked Jamie, "What is that sign doing in the yard?" She said, "The landlord came by and said we have to be out November first."

God didn't give me direction by a booming voice that echoed down from the heavens, saying, "Thus saith the Lord, thou shalt leave Seagoville, Texas." No, I just lost my desire to be there. This is one of the ways God speaks to us—through the desires of our hearts.

One of the reasons that some people aren't satisfied with getting up and going to work, coming home, watching television, going to bed, and then getting up and doing the whole thing over again is because they aren't doing what God called them to do. It's a holy dissatisfaction. You are never going to have the sense of joy and peace that I've been talking about until you get in line with God's will for your life. Unless you are doing what God created you to do, you will never have the drive that continually wakes you up in the morning excited about life, knowing that you are on a path that is making a difference and changing others.

It's sad to say, but a lot of Christians have never known the satisfaction that comes from being in the center of God's will. One of the reasons for this is because the church has been more *influenced* by the world than *influencing* the world.

Many of us were raised, whether in a Christian home or not, to think that our lives are our own, and we can do whatever we want with them. Still others grew up thinking they were a mistake because their parents told them they were the result of an unplanned pregnancy. Some look around and feel like they missed out on the talents and abilities they see in others. In one way or another, many people go through life feeling like they are a mistake—so they just struggle and try to cope the best they can.

The Lord's plan for your life is far better than that. You aren't a mistake. You didn't miss out on the talents you need to accomplish God's will. You don't have to struggle through life, bouncing from one crisis to the next. God has a purpose for you. He created you for a reason. You have a specific purpose in life, and God wants you to discover what that purpose is.

Separated from the Womb

I praise you because I am fearfully and wonderfully made; your works are wonderful, I know that full well. [15] My frame was not hidden from you when

I was made in the secret place. When I was woven together in the depths of the earth, [16] your eyes saw my unformed body. All the days ordained for me were written in your book before one of them came to be. [17] How precious to me are your thoughts, O God! How vast is the sum of them!
PSALM 139:14-17, NEW INTERNATIONAL VERSION 1984

What a tremendous passage of Scripture! God saw you before you were ever born. He saw you in your mother's womb. At the same time you were being physically formed, God wove in your talents, abilities, and purpose. It's a part of who you are. Before you were even born, God had already written down what your life is supposed to be. He had written down your talents and abilities.

You may think you made yourself an artist, or an accountant, or whatever it is that you are, but *you can't bring out what God didn't put in.* God gave you a disposition. He gave you a certain inclination. Some people are vivacious and lively, while others are quiet and reserved. God gave you the personality you have. He made you the way you are. You can change to a degree, but you can't change the *core* of who you are.

I used to be a runner, but now I'm a walker. In high school, they tried to make me run sprints—fifty-yard dashes. I did it, but I hated it and was never really good at it. I was good enough to make the track team but never good enough to win any medals. After I finished school, I started jogging and discovered that I loved to jog. I enjoyed running fifteen or twenty miles slowly, but running fifty yards as fast as I could really bothered me.

I eventually learned that muscles are made up of fast-twitch and slow-twitch fibers. Sprinters have a majority of fast-twitch muscle fibers, while distance runners have more slow-twitch muscle fibers. You can change the ratio of fast-twitch to slow-twitch fibers in your muscles through training, but not by much. The basic balance doesn't change. Some people are built for speed; others are built for endurance. I didn't like sprinting, because I wasn't built to run sprints. I was built for long-distance running.

In the same way, your personality can be influenced and changed to a degree, but you have a genetic disposition to be a certain type of person with a certain type of personality. You were designed that way. Before you were formed, God had already planned those things. He had it written out. He wove in your abilities and purpose, but He won't force His will for your life to come to pass.

This is something that keeps people from finding and recognizing God's will for their lives. They have a fatalistic attitude that whatever is meant to be, will be—like that old song,

"Que sera, sera. Whatever will be, will be." If you let fate dictate your life, you will make a lot of wrong decisions. You can't just let circumstances move and control you. God doesn't move you around like a pawn. Many think that God is sovereign and whatever His will is comes to pass, but that isn't how it works.

God is sovereign in the sense that He has supreme power and is Master of all things, seen and unseen. But He is not sovereign in the sense that nothing can happen without His permission. God doesn't control your life. He doesn't force His will to come to pass. Everything that happens in your life is not God's will. I know a lot of people teach that nothing can happen unless God wills it to happen, but that isn't what the Word of God says. For example, the Apostle Peter wrote,

> *The Lord is not slack concerning his promise, as some men count slackness; but is longsuffering to us-ward, not willing that any should perish, but that all should come to repentance.*
>
> 2 PETER 3:9

It's very clear that God doesn't want anyone to miss out on salvation. He desires for everyone to receive salvation, yet Jesus said there would be more people who perish by entering the broad gate that leads to destruction than those who are saved by entering through the narrow gate that leads to everlasting life (Matt. 7:13-14). God wants every person to be saved, yet not everyone will be saved. Jesus even prophesied that not everyone will be saved.

The reason God's will does not automatically come to pass in our lives is that we have a part to play. We choose whether or not we will be saved by our response to Jesus. We have a choice in the matter. In the same way, God has a plan for you, but you have control over your own life. God is not going to make His will come to pass in your life without your cooperation.

Before you were born, before you were even formed in the womb, God had a plan for your life. You were born a man or a woman, at this time in history, in the nation you were born in for a reason. It isn't a coincidence. God chose you. He has a purpose for you, and He gave you gifts and abilities to accomplish that purpose. God created you for a reason and has a specific plan for what He wants you to do, but ultimately *you* are in control.

Steps and Stages

If you feel like a square peg in a round hole, it might be because you have allowed circumstances to move you away from the direction God has planned for you. The reason you aren't satisfied or fulfilled is that you aren't moving in the right direction. You will never have the degree of success you could have in life until you first find God's will.

When I first started seeking the Lord, I knew I was called to minister, but I didn't know in what capacity. Over a period of time, I discovered that I was called to teach—as opposed to being an evangelist. My gifting was toward the body of Christ, to help believers learn who they are in Christ. Initially, however, I didn't know exactly what area of ministry I was called to, so I started out by holding Bible studies. This was back before there was such a thing as a Spirit-filled church. People thought that if you spoke in tongues, you were of the devil. I actually made a top ten list of things that were "of the devil" in my town—I was number one on the list!

All of the people who came to my Bible studies were kicked out of their churches, so they said, "We're going to start tithing here. This is our church now."

"Wait a second," I told them. "This isn't a church—it's a Bible study. And I'm not a pastor."

"Well, you can call it whatever you want to," they said, "but we don't have anywhere else to go. This is where we go, so you're our pastor."

I became a pastor by default. I didn't want to be a pastor. I never felt called to be a pastor. But the people in my Bible study started calling me "Pastor," and I ended up pastoring three churches. God used me in that role: lives were changed, people were born again, and good things happened—but it wasn't my calling.

After I started on radio, I held my first Gospel meeting when I advertised the event during my broadcast and invited everyone who could make it. It was awesome! After the very first meeting, I knew that I was made to travel and minister in exactly that way. Even though I had been teaching the same things before, I felt a new sense of liberty, satisfaction, and joy when I started ministering in the way God created me to.

I wasn't out of His will when I was pastoring those three churches—it was a time of training for me. God taught me during that period and I learned a lot, but I wasn't yet in the *center* of His will. You don't go from *not* being in God's will to instantly being *in* the center of His will. It's a process. It takes time; it happens progressively.

I started ministering in 1968. On July 26, 1999, the Lord woke me up in the middle of the night and spoke to me about some things. He told me I was just then beginning to fulfill what He had called me to do, and if I had died before then, I would have missed His perfect will for my life. It was both *discouraging* and *encouraging* at the same time to hear those things.

It was discouraging because I had been ministering for thirty-one years and had seen great things happen, but the Lord was telling me that I was just then getting to the center of His will. But it also encouraged me because I was already seeing God do wonderful things and felt extremely blessed to be doing what He had called me to do. I thought, *If I'm just now getting closer to doing what God called me to do, then it's going to get even better!* And it has. Our ministry has grown extensively, and we're reaching more people than ever with the Gospel. I have to run to keep up. It's awesome! But we didn't get here overnight.

The reason you might find life hard or are not experiencing satisfaction is because God created you to do something different from what you are doing. He created you for one thing, and you are off doing something else. Maybe you just fell into what you are doing; you were recruited at a college career day or got married and took whatever opportunity you could. Life might have just kind of taken a path on its own, which happens. But I hope you recognize now that God created you for a unique purpose and that you have to intentionally pursue that purpose.

V.   When you aren't going in the right direction, He will sometimes turn you around by giving you a sense of unrest, or what I call a "holy dissatisfaction."

   A.   The dissatisfaction that God uses to give direction to believers who are seeking Him is completely different from the turmoil of negative emotions.

   B.   God doesn't use depression to guide you—one of the ways He speaks to you is through the desires of your heart.

   C.   One of the reasons that some people aren't satisfied with getting up and going to work, coming home, watching television, going to bed, and then getting up and doing the whole thing over again is because they aren't doing what God called them to do.

   D.   You need to know that you are on a path that is making a difference and changing others.

VI.   Many people were raised, whether in a Christian home or not, to think that their lives are their own, and they can do whatever they want with them.

   A.   The Lord's plan for your life is far better than that.

   B.   You aren't a mistake, you didn't miss out on the talents you need to accomplish God's will, and you don't have to struggle through life, bouncing from one crisis to the next.

   C.   You have a specific purpose in life, and God wants you to discover what that purpose is.

VII.   At the same time you were being physically formed, God wove in your talents, abilities, and purpose.

   I praise you because I am fearfully and wonderfully made; your works are wonderful, I know that full well. [15] My frame was not hidden from you when I was made in the secret place. When I was woven together in the depths of the earth, [16] your eyes saw my unformed body. All the days ordained for me were written in your book before one of them came to be. [17] How precious to me are your thoughts, O God! How vast is the sum of them!
   PSALM 139:14-17, NEW INTERNATIONAL VERSION 1984

   A.   Before you were even born, God had already written down what your life is supposed to be.

   B.   You may think you made yourself, but you can't bring out what God didn't put in.

   C.   God gave you a disposition.

   D.   Some people are vivacious and lively, while others are quiet and reserved.

   E.   Your personality can be influenced and changed to a degree, but you have a genetic disposition to be a certain type of person with a certain type of personality.

VIII. God won't force His will for your life to come to pass.

    A. One of the things that keeps people from finding and recognizing God's will for their lives is a fatalistic attitude that whatever is meant to be, will be.

    B. You can't just let circumstances move and control you.

    C. Many think that whatever God's will is comes to pass, but that isn't how it works.

    D. God is sovereign in the sense that He has supreme power and is Master of all things, seen and unseen, but He is not sovereign in the sense that nothing can happen without His permission.

    E. Everything that happens in your life is not God's will.

    F. For example, God wants every person to be saved, yet not everyone will be saved (2 Pet. 3:9 and Matt. 7:13-14).

IX. The reason God's will does not automatically come to pass in your life is that you have a part to play.

    A. You choose whether or not you will be saved by your response to Jesus.

    B. In the same way, God has a plan for you, but you have control over your own life.

    C. You were born a man or a woman, at this time in history, in the nation you were born in for a reason—it isn't a coincidence.

    D. God chose you.

    E. He has a purpose for you, and He gave you gifts and abilities to accomplish that purpose.

X. If you feel like a square peg in a round hole, it might be because you have allowed circumstances to move you away from the direction God has planned for you.

    A. You will never have the degree of success you could have in life until you first find God's will.

    B. When I first started seeking the Lord, I knew I was called to minister, but I didn't know in what capacity.

        i. Over a period of time, I discovered that I was called to teach—my gifting was toward the body of Christ, to help believers learn who they are in Christ.

        ii. Initially, however, I didn't know exactly what area of ministry I was called to.

        iii. But after I held my first Gospel meeting, I knew that I was made to travel and minister in exactly that way.

        iv. I felt a new sense of liberty, satisfaction, and joy when I started ministering in the way God created me to.

C. God taught me during that period and I learned a lot, but I wasn't yet in the *center* of His will.

D. You don't go from *not* being in God's will to instantly being *in* the center of His will—it's a process and happens progressively.

XI. One night, the Lord woke me up and told me I was just then beginning to fulfill what He had called me to do, and if I had died before then, I would have missed His perfect will for my life.

A. It was discouraging to hear that, because I had been ministering for thirty-one years and had seen great things happen.

B. But it also encouraged me because I was already seeing God do wonderful things and felt extremely blessed to be doing what He had called me to do.

C. Since then, our ministry has grown extensively, and we're reaching more people than ever with the Gospel, but we didn't get here overnight.

XII. The reason you might find life hard or are not experiencing satisfaction is because God created you to do something different from what you are doing.

A. Maybe you just fell into what you are doing.

B. Life might have just kind of taken a path on its own, which happens.

C. But I hope you recognize now that God created you for a unique purpose and that you have to intentionally pursue that purpose.

5. When you aren't going in the right direction, God will sometimes turn you around by giving you a sense of unrest, or what I call a "holy dissatisfaction." The dissatisfaction that God uses to give direction to believers who are seeking Him is completely different from the turmoil of negative emotions. God doesn't use depression to guide you—one of the ways He speaks to you is through the desires of your heart. One of the reasons that some people aren't satisfied with getting up and going to work, coming home, watching television, going to bed, and then getting up and doing the whole thing over again is because they aren't doing what God called them to do. You need to know that you are on a path that is making a difference and changing others.

5a.   Discussion question: How would you describe a holy dissatisfaction?
Discussion question

5b.   "A sense of unrest" is not to be confused with what?
      A. "Pressure from friends to do what they think is best"
      B. "Having difficulty sleeping at night"
      C. "The turmoil that comes from negative emotions"
      D. "Favorable circumstances"
      E. "Unfavorable circumstances"
      C. "The turmoil that comes from negative emotions"

5c.   Discussion question: When you experience a holy dissatisfaction, how does God speak to you through the desires of your heart?
Discussion question

6. Many people were raised, whether in a Christian home or not, to think that their lives are their own, and they can do whatever they want with them. The Lord's plan for your life is far better than that. You aren't a mistake, you didn't miss out on the talents you need to accomplish God's will, and you don't have to struggle through life, bouncing from one crisis to the next. You have a specific purpose in life, and God wants you to discover what that purpose is.

6a.   Discussion question: Why do you suppose there are Christians who think their lives are their own, and they can do whatever they want with them?
Discussion question

6b.   True or false: You didn't miss out on the talents you need to accomplish God's will.
      True

6c.   True or false: There will be times in life when you will have to bounce from one crisis to the next.
      False

7. At the same time you were being physically formed, God wove in your talents, abilities, and purpose.

> *I praise you because I am fearfully and wonderfully made; your works are wonderful, I know that full well. [15] My frame was not hidden from you when I was made in the secret place. When I was woven together in the depths of the earth, [16] your eyes saw my unformed body. All the days ordained for me were written in your book before one of them came to be. [17] How precious to me are your thoughts, O God! How vast is the sum of them!*
> PSALM 139:14-17, NEW INTERNATIONAL VERSION 1984

Before you were even born, God had already written down what your life is supposed to be. You may think you made yourself, but you can't bring out what God didn't put in. God gave you a disposition. Some people are vivacious and lively, while others are quiet and reserved. Your personality can be influenced and changed to a degree, but you have a genetic disposition to be a certain type of person with a certain type of personality.

7a. Read Psalm 139:14-17. At the time you were being physically formed, what did God weave in?
Your talents, abilities, and purpose

7b. If you think you made yourself, what don't you realize?
A. That you're not the only one
B. That you can't bring out what God didn't put in
C. That you're really only a product of your environment
D. All of the above
E. None of the above
B. That you can't bring out what God didn't put in

7c. You have a _____ disposition to be a certain type of person with a certain type of personality.
Genetic

8. God won't force His will for your life to come to pass. One of the things that keeps people from finding and recognizing God's will for their lives is a fatalistic attitude that whatever is meant to be, will be. You can't just let circumstances move and control you. Many think that whatever God's will is comes to pass, but that isn't how it works. God is sovereign in the sense that He has supreme power and is Master of all things, seen and unseen, but He is not sovereign in the sense that nothing can happen without His permission. Everything that happens in your life is not God's will. For example, God wants every person to be saved, yet not everyone will be saved (2 Pet. 3:9 and Matt. 7:13-14).

8a.   True or false: God will force His will for your life to come to pass.
False

8b.   What's one thing that keeps people from finding and recognizing God's will for their lives?
A fatalistic attitude that whatever is meant to be, will be

8c.   God is not _____ in the sense that nothing can happen without His permission.
Sovereign

8d.   Read 2 Peter 3:9 and Matthew 7:13-14. What do these two passages prove?
That God every person to be saved, yet not everyone will be saved

9. The reason God's will does not automatically come to pass in your life is that you have a part to play. You choose whether or not you will be saved by your response to Jesus. In the same way, God has a plan for you, but you have control over your own life. You were born a man or a woman, at this time in history, in the nation you were born in for a reason—it isn't a coincidence. God chose you. He has a purpose for you, and He gave you gifts and abilities to accomplish that purpose.

9a.   Why doesn't God's will automatically come to pass in your life?
  A. Because God doesn't think you're holy enough
  B. Because people hinder God's will
  C. Because you have too much unbelief
  D. Because you don't have enough money
  E. Because you have a part to play
  E. Because you have a part to play

9b.   Discussion question: Though you have control over your own life, what should you do with it?
Discussion question

10. If you feel like a square peg in a round hole, it might be because you have allowed circumstances to move you away from the direction God has planned for you. You will never have the degree of success you could have in life until you first find God's will. When I first started seeking the Lord, I knew I was called to minister, but I didn't know in what capacity. Over a period of time, I discovered that I was called to teach—my gifting was toward the body of Christ, to help believers learn who they are in Christ. Initially, however, I didn't know exactly what area of ministry I was called to. But after I held my first Gospel meeting, I knew that I was made to travel and minister in exactly that way. I felt a new sense of liberty, satisfaction, and joy when I started ministering in the way God created me to. God taught me during that period and I learned a lot, but I wasn't yet in the *center* of His will. You don't go from *not* being in God's will to instantly being *in* the center of His will—it's a process and happens progressively.

10a. You will never have the degree of _____ you could have in life until you first find God's will.
Success

10b. What did Andrew feel after he held his first Gospel meeting?
A new sense of liberty, satisfaction, and joy

10c. What does it take to be in the center of God's will?
   A. A successful fundraiser
   B. Time and progression
   C. Agreement from family
   D. All of the above
   E. None of the above
   B. Time and progression

11. One night, the Lord woke me up and told me I was just then beginning to fulfill what He had called me to do, and if I had died before then, I would have missed His perfect will for my life. It was discouraging to hear that, because I had been ministering for thirty-one years and had seen great things happen. But it also encouraged me because I was already seeing God do wonderful things and felt extremely blessed to be doing what He had called me to do. Since then, our ministry has grown extensively, and we're reaching more people than ever with the Gospel, but we didn't get here overnight.

11a. Discussion question: What do you think your response would be if God had told you what He told Andrew?
Discussion question

12. The reason you might find life hard or are not experiencing satisfaction is because God created you to do something different from what you are doing. Maybe you just fell into what you are doing. Life might have just kind of taken a path on its own, which happens. But I hope you recognize now that God created you for a unique purpose and that you have to intentionally pursue that purpose.

12a. The reason you might find life hard or are not experiencing satisfaction is because God _____ you to do something different from what you are doing.
   Created

12b. God created you for a unique purpose, but you have to do what?
   A. Start making friends
   B. Intentionally pursue that purpose
   C. Do whatever a church leader advises
   D. Take out a loan
   E. Sell everything you own
   B. Intentionally pursue that purpose

16. Discussion question: How would you describe a holy dissatisfaction?

_____

_____

_____

17. "A sense of unrest" is not to be confused with what?
    A. "Pressure from friends to do what they think is best"
    B. "Having difficulty sleeping at night"
    C. "The turmoil that comes from negative emotions"
    D. "Favorable circumstances"
    E. "Unfavorable circumstances"

18. Discussion question: When you experience a holy dissatisfaction, how does God speak to you through the desires of your heart?

_____

_____

_____

19. Discussion question: Why do you suppose there are Christians who think their lives are their own, and they can do whatever they want with them?

_____

_____

_____

20. True or false: You didn't miss out on the talents you need to accomplish God's will.

21. True or false: There will be times in life when you will have to bounce from one crisis to the next.

22. Read Psalm 139:14-17. At the time you were being physically formed, what did God weave in?

_____

_____

_____

23. If you think you made yourself, what don't you realize?
    A. That you're not the only one
    B. That you can't bring out what God didn't put in
    C. That you're really only a product of your environment
    D. All of the above
    E. None of the above

24. You have a _____ disposition to be a certain type of person with a certain type of personality.

25. True or false: God will force His will for your life to come to pass.

26. What's one thing that keeps people from finding and recognizing God's will for their lives?

_____

_____

_____

27. God is not _____ in the sense that nothing can happen without His permission.

28. Read 2 Peter 3:9 and Matthew 7:13-14. What do these two passages prove?

_____

_____

_____

29. Why doesn't God's will automatically come to pass in your life?
    A. Because God doesn't think you're holy enough
    B. Because people hinder God's will
    C. Because you have too much unbelief
    D. Because you don't have enough money
    E. Because you have a part to play

30. Discussion question: Though you have control over your own life, what should you do with it?

_____

_____

_____

31. You will never have the degree of _____ you could have in life until you first find God's will.

32. What did Andrew feel after he held his first Gospel meeting?

_____

_____

_____

33. What does it take to be in the center of God's will?
    A. A successful fundraiser
    B. Time and progression
    C. Agreement from family
    D. All of the above
    E. None of the above

34. Discussion question: What do you think your response would be if God had told you what He told Andrew?

_____

_____

_____

35. The reason you might find life hard or are not experiencing satisfaction is because God _____ you to do something different from what you are doing.

36. God created you for a unique purpose, but you have to do what?
    A. Start making friends
    B. Intentionally pursue that purpose
    C. Do whatever a church leader advises
    D. Take out a loan
    E. Sell everything you own

16. *Discussion question*

17. C. "The turmoil that comes from negative emotions"

18. *Discussion question*

19. *Discussion question*

20. True

21. False

22. Your talents, abilities, and purpose

23. B. That you can't bring out what God didn't put in

24. Genetic

25. False

26. A fatalistic attitude that whatever is meant to be, will be

27. Sovereign

28. That God every person to be saved, yet not everyone will be saved

29. E. Because you have a part to play

30. *Discussion question*

31. Success

32. A new sense of liberty, satisfaction, and joy

33. B. Time and progression

34. *Discussion question*

35. Created

36. B. Intentionally pursue that purpose

ROMANS 8:6

For to be carnally minded is death; but to be spiritually minded is life and peace.

PSALM 139:14-17, *NEW INTERNATIONAL VERSION 1984*

I praise you because I am fearfully and wonderfully made; your works are wonderful, I know that full well. [15] My frame was not hidden from you when I was made in the secret place. When I was woven together in the depths of the earth, [16] your eyes saw my unformed body. All the days ordained for me were written in your book before one of them came to be. [17] How precious to me are your thoughts, O God! How vast is the sum of them!

2 PETER 3:9

The Lord is not slack concerning his promise, as some men count slackness; but is longsuffering to us-ward, not willing that any should perish, but that all should come to repentance.

MATTHEW 7:13-14

Enter ye in at the strait gate: for wide is the gate, and broad is the way, that leadeth to destruction, and many there be which go in thereat: [14] Because strait is the gate, and narrow is the way, which leadeth unto life, and few there be that find it.

LESSON 1.3

For ye have heard of my conversation in time past in the Jews' religion, how that beyond measure I persecuted the church of God, and wasted it: [14] And profited in the Jews' religion above many my equals in mine own nation, being more exceedingly zealous of the traditions of my fathers. [15] But when it pleased God, who separated me from my mother's womb, and called me by his grace.

GALATIANS 1:13-15

When the Apostle Paul wrote that God had *"separated"* him, he meant that God had "set him apart" for a specific purpose. God set Paul apart from his mother's womb to preach the Gospel. This is a radical thought. We always look at a person's qualifications when we are trying to fill a position in church or in the workplace. We want to know if the applicant is reliable. We look at their accomplishments and natural abilities and essentially choose people based on their past performance. But God's way is different.

This passage of Scripture says that God chose Paul and set him apart from his mother's womb to preach the Gospel—before he ever did anything good or bad or developed his talents and abilities. God isn't looking at your resumé and saying, "Oh, look at what you've accomplished. You would be a great choice. I think I'll call you to do this." No, God doesn't work like that. *From the very moment of conception, God had a plan, and from your mother's womb, God already had a purpose designed for you.*

Our talents and abilities can be an indication of God's will, but many of us have hidden talents and gifts that we have never recognized or developed. If we only look at what we *think* our talents and abilities are, we will miss God. We won't see our real potential until we get beyond ourselves and get into a realm of trusting God for something supernatural. We can't just say, "Well, I've always been able to speak in front of people, so maybe God wants me to be a preacher or something like that." We aren't going to find God's will that way.

I used to be someone who couldn't look other people in the face and speak to them. I remember walking down the street one day when I was a senior in high school, and a man walked past me and said, "Good morning." He was two blocks down the street before I let out my response, "Good morning, sir."

I got into my car and sat there thinking, *God, what is wrong with me?* I was so introverted. Looking at my natural qualifications up to that point, the last thing you would think I would ever end up doing is speaking in front of thousands of people. But God has called me to do something totally *contrary* to my nature.

God has changed me, but I still like being alone. I really enjoy it. When I want to have a great time, I'll go spend some time by myself—that's my nature. God called me to do something opposite from my natural inclination. Too many people are trying to figure out what to do with their lives by looking at their natural abilities—or worse, at the results of a personality test. A test can't tell you what God's plan for your life is. A personality test can give you a snapshot of where you are at the time you take the test, but the results aren't true forever.

If I would have taken a personality test before God touched me in 1968, I guarantee you I would have tested as an extreme *introvert*. But if I took that same test today, I'd test as a maximum *extrovert*. A test is just a snapshot of where you are. It may tell you what your personality type is like at that moment, but it can't tell you God's real plan and purpose for your life. Some people have been so wounded and beaten into submission by life that the snapshot isn't going to give them a true indication of their potential.

God didn't look at Paul when he was twenty or thirty years old and say, "Wow, you've spent twenty years studying under Gamaliel and have all of this knowledge under your belt, so I think I'll use you to preach the Gospel and write half the New Testament." God doesn't operate that way. As a matter of fact, most of us would have picked Peter to go to the heathen—he was half heathen himself. When Jesus called Peter, he was probably out there in the boat, cussing. Peter had an attitude. It seemed like the only time he opened his mouth was to change feet! He was always doing something wrong.

Peter wasn't polished or religious, so most of us would have thought he'd have been a great guy to send to the heathen—and we would have sent Paul to the Jews! Paul was schooled in the Jewish religion—he knew the Law frontward and backward. He also had a revelation of grace. Who better to convince a legalistic Jew than Paul? He was the greatest Pharisee of them all. Yet God sent Paul to preach to the heathen and Peter to preach to the legalistic Jews.

You might be thinking, *God couldn't use me; I've been mediocre my whole life.* But God doesn't plan His purposes for your life according to your previous achievements. He will always call you to do something that is beyond your natural ability, forcing you to rely on Him. If you only do what you feel you are naturally equipped to do—what you are capable of doing in your own strength and ability—then you will be tempted to give yourself the credit for success. You'll think, *I'm really good at this; I'm just a natural.* In fact, I would say that if you are simply doing what comes naturally to you, then you probably haven't found God's will for your life yet.

God separated Paul from his mother's womb, before he had honed his skills or accomplished anything in life. Likewise, God's purpose for you may or may not be in accordance with what you perceive as your strengths. I've heard it said that the place with the most potential on earth is a graveyard, because most people die without reaching their potential—they take it to the grave.

You were separated from the womb, and God put abilities in you to fulfill His purposes. But He is not going to make His will come to pass without your cooperation. You have to make an effort to find God's plan for your life. You can't judge what His plan is by merely looking at your natural abilities. If you look at your history of successes or failures, you might miss God's plan and never realize the potential He has placed inside of you.

Not Everything that's Good Is God

Major life changes can be unsettling to contemplate, especially if you have a career and things are going well or if you are thinking about retirement and looking forward to coasting for a while. You don't want any bumps in the road. Yet here I am asking, "Have you really found the purpose God has for you?" No matter how unpleasant the thought of change may seem, it is important to know whether or not you have found your life's purpose.

I believe that most people have not found God's will for their lives. Most people are not accomplishing what God created them to do. They may be doing something good, but just because it's good doesn't mean it's God. Not everything that is good is God's will. You may be an accomplished professional doing wonderful things, but are you doing what God has called you to do?

We each only have one chance to fulfill God's will for our lives. God's intention is not that we do whatever we want to with our lives and then, as long as our hearts are pure, everything will be all right. No, you were created by God for a specific purpose that you are not going to fulfill accidentally. You have to get a revelation of what God's will is and then swim upstream to pursue it. Only with effort and time will you see God's will for your life come to pass. It isn't going to happen by fate. You have to take charge of your life and pursue God's will. You have to take control!

Find out where God wants you to go and steer your life in that direction. Jamie and I are exactly where God wants us to be, doing what He wants us to do, but we wouldn't be in the center of His will today if we had taken the easy road in the past. *"Que sera, sera"* isn't a philosophy that gets great results in life. We have sought God. We have stood against circumstances and situations that have tried to turn us away from God's will. We had to persevere. We didn't get where we are by accident or by our own strength and wisdom. It took effort. Without work and determination, I don't believe you will be able to reach the center of God's will either.

Paul said of himself, *"It pleased God, who separated me from my mother's womb, and called me by his grace"* (Gal. 1:15). Paul recognized that the Lord had a purpose for him in being a representative of God. Yet for twenty or thirty years of his life, he thought that being a legalistic Jew was the way he would fulfill God's will. Paul said he was more zealous than anybody else and profited in the Jew's religion above many of his equals (Gal. 1:14). Finally, the Lord revealed Himself miraculously and said *"You're doing it all wrong,"* and Paul had to completely reverse the direction his life was going.

Paul's life is proof that merely discovering some of your talents doesn't necessarily mean that you are using them in the way God intends for you to use them. Maybe you are—but you need to hear from God to be sure. You need to find out. Life is not a dress rehearsal; it's the real deal. You will never have another today. You have to make every day count. You have to spend every day moving in the direction that God wants your life to go. You don't have time to meander through life, hoping to stumble into your purpose or praying that in the end, God will use you.

It's so easy to get established in a routine. When we get a little bit of security and the pressure is off, we want to put life on cruise control. It can feel a little threatening to get out of a routine and do something new, especially if we have been doing the same thing for a long time. But we have to be willing to get out of our comfort zones in order to find God's purpose for our lives. I promise, knowing the joy of being in the center of God's will makes it all worthwhile.

God called me to teach and minister to people. I'm doing what God has called me to do. I can name tons of people who have been healed, marriages that have been restored, and people who have been born again. It has been awesome! But you don't have to be a minister to have a God-given purpose. The Lord has a unique purpose for everyone.

I spend millions of dollars on radio and television, yet there are people you know—friends, relatives, neighbors—who will never hear of me. It wouldn't matter if I spent ten times as much money as I am spending right now, because there would still be certain people who would never hear me preach the Gospel. Some of those people might be your friends and neighbors. An ordained minister might never reach them, but you could.

You have miracles that God has appointed for you to carry out. You may never be on radio or television, and God may not use you to speak in front of thousands of people, but you have a sphere of influence—people in your life—that might never receive the full anointing God has for them unless you reach your potential. You don't have to mature as a Christian before God will love you. God's love is unconditional, and He accepts you right where you are. But you will be happier and a much greater blessing to the people in your life once you find your purpose and start heading in that direction.

It's possible that God wants you in the very business you're in. Not everyone who wants to live for God needs to become a full-time minister. We need believers who are out in the world, functioning in the power of God and His gifts. Becoming a pastor isn't the only way to serve God. In fact, God calls more people into business and labor than He calls into full-time ministry. Regardless of what you are called to do, God wants you to reach people and manifest His power in the world.

You need to know that you are doing what God made you for, not simply hoping that you are doing something that is acceptable to Him. I think it would be terrible to live your whole life and not know for sure that you are doing what God created you to do. I can't imagine what that would be like. It would terrify me to go to bed and wake up not having a clue if I am following God's will.

The only thing worse than not knowing God's will is knowing His will and choosing not to do it—either because you have talked yourself out of it or have let others talk you out of it. To know that God made you for a purpose and to feel unqualified or incapable of fulfilling it, is worse than not knowing at all.

It motivates me to know that I am doing what God created me to do. I get up in the morning with a purpose. I know I haven't achieved all that God has planned for me, but I'm progressing in the right direction. A God-given purpose and a life driven by the Holy Spirit motivate me to work through life's hardships. I don't know how people who live without a purpose find the incentive to muddle through—other than knowing that the alternative is worse. Going to work because it beats starving to death is a terrible way to live your life. You need to know that you're doing what God has called you to do. You need to live your life on purpose.

God has a purpose for every person alive. I don't care if your parents liked you or wanted you. God knew you were coming. God wrote down everything about you in His book, and He has a plan for you. Every gift and talent, the time you were born, the country you were born in, and everything else about you was designed by God. You are not an accident. God has a perfect plan for your life, and His plan is better than your plan for yourself.

XIII. Galatians 1:13-15 says that God chose Paul and set him apart from his mother's womb to preach the Gospel—before he ever did anything good or bad or developed his talents and abilities.

A. *From the very moment of conception, God had a plan, and from your mother's womb, God already had a purpose designed for you.*

B. Your talents and abilities can be an indication of God's will, but many have hidden talents and gifts that they have never recognized or developed.

C. You won't see your real potential until you get beyond yourself and get into a realm of trusting God for something supernatural.

D. Too many people are trying to figure out what to do with their lives by looking at their natural abilities—or worse, at the results of a personality test.

E. A personality test can give you a snapshot of where you are at the time you take the test, but the results aren't true forever—and it can't tell you God's real plan and purpose for your life.

F. God didn't look at Paul when he was twenty or thirty years old and say, "Wow, you've spent twenty years studying under Gamaliel and have all of this knowledge under your belt, so I think I'll use you to preach the Gospel and write half the New Testament."

G. Paul was schooled in the Jewish religion—he knew the Law frontward and backward, and he also had a revelation of grace—so who better to convince a legalistic Jew than Paul?

H. Peter wasn't polished or religious, so most would have thought he'd have been a great guy to send to the heathen.

I. Yet God sent Paul to preach to the heathen and Peter to preach to the legalistic Jews.

J. God will always call you to do something that is beyond your natural ability, forcing you to rely on Him.

K. If you only do what you feel you are naturally equipped to do—what you are capable of doing in your own strength and ability—then you will be tempted to give yourself the credit for success.

L. In fact, if you are simply doing what comes naturally to you, then you probably haven't found God's will for your life yet.

XIV. Major life changes can be unsettling to contemplate, especially if you have a career and things are going well or if you are thinking about retirement and looking forward to coasting for a while.

A. No matter how unpleasant the thought of change may seem, it is important to know whether or not you have found your life's purpose.

B. You only have one chance to fulfill God's will for your life.

C. God's intention is not that you do whatever you want with your life and then, as long as your heart is pure, everything will be all right.

D. Only with effort and time will you see God's will for your life come to pass.

E. You have to take charge of your life and pursue God's will.

XV. You will never have another today.

A. You have to spend every day moving in the direction that God wants your life to go.

B. It can feel a little threatening to get out of a routine and do something new, especially if we have been doing the same thing for a long time, but you have to be willing to get out of your comfort zone in order to find God's purpose for your life.

C. I promise, knowing the joy of being in the center of God's will makes it all worthwhile.

XVI. There are certain people who would never hear me preach the Gospel.

A. You have a sphere of influence—people in your life—that might never receive the full anointing God has for them unless you reach your potential.

B. You will be happier and a much greater blessing to the people in your life once you find your purpose and start heading in that direction.

C. God calls more people into business and labor than He calls into full-time ministry.

D. Regardless of what you are called to do, God wants you to reach people and manifest His power in the world.

XVII. I think it would be terrible to live your whole life and not know for sure that you are doing what God created you to do.

A. It would terrify me to go to bed and wake up not having a clue if I am following God's will.

B. The only thing worse than not knowing God's will is knowing His will and choosing not to do it—either because you have talked yourself out of it or have let others talk you out of it.

C. To know that God made you for a purpose and to feel unqualified or incapable of fulfilling it, is worse than not knowing at all.

D. A God-given purpose and a life driven by the Holy Spirit motivate me to work through life's hardships.

E. Going to work because it beats starving to death is a terrible way to live your life.

F. You need to live your life on purpose.

G. God has a perfect plan for your life, and His plan is better than your plan for yourself.

13. Galatians 1:13-15 says that God chose Paul and set him apart from his mother's womb to preach the Gospel—before he ever did anything good or bad or developed his talents and abilities. *From the very moment of conception, God had a plan, and from your mother's womb, God already had a purpose designed for you.* Your talents and abilities can be an indication of God's will, but many have hidden talents and gifts that they have never recognized or developed. You won't see your real potential until you get beyond yourself and get into a realm of trusting God for something supernatural. Too many people are trying to figure out what to do with their lives by looking at their natural abilities—or worse, at the results of a personality test. A personality test can give you a snapshot of where you are at the time you take the test, but the results aren't true forever—and it can't tell you God's real plan and purpose for your life. God didn't look at Paul when he was twenty or thirty years old and say, "Wow, you've spent twenty years studying under Gamaliel and have all of this knowledge under your belt, so I think I'll use you to preach the Gospel and write half the New Testament." Paul was schooled in the Jewish religion—he knew the Law frontward and backward, and he also had a revelation of grace—so who better to convince a legalistic Jew than Paul? Peter wasn't polished or religious, so most would have thought he'd have been a great guy to send to the heathen. Yet God sent Paul to preach to the heathen and Peter to preach to the legalistic Jews. God will always call you to do something that is beyond your natural ability, forcing you to rely on Him. If you only do what you feel you are naturally equipped to do—what you are capable of doing in your own strength and ability—then you will be tempted to give yourself the credit for success. In fact, if you are simply doing what comes naturally to you, then you probably haven't found God's will for your life yet.

13a. Discussion question: What do you think about the fact that God had a plan and purpose for you before you were born?
Discussion question

13b. Too many people are trying to figure out what to do with their lives by looking at what?
   A. The new charismatic televangelist
   B. What they see other people doing
   C. Circumstances working out a certain way
   D. Their natural abilities or a personality test
   E. The money in their bank accounts
   D. Their natural abilities or a personality test

13c. Why aren't the results of a personality test true forever?
Because they only give you a snapshot of where you are at the time you take the test

13d. True or false: Personality tests can't tell you God's real plan and purpose for your life.
True

13e. Discussion question: Why do you think God will always call you to do something that is beyond your natural ability, forcing you to rely on Him?
Discussion question

13f. If you only do what you feel you are naturally equipped to do—what you are capable of doing in your own strength and ability—then you will be tempted to give
_____ the credit for success.
Yourself

14. Major life changes can be unsettling to contemplate, especially if you have a career and things are going well or if you are thinking about retirement and looking forward to coasting for a while. No matter how unpleasant the thought of change may seem, it is important to know whether or not you have found your life's purpose. You only have one chance to fulfill God's will for your life. God's intention is not that you do whatever you want with your life and then, as long as your heart is pure, everything will be all right. Only with effort and time will you see God's will for your life come to pass. You have to take charge of your life and pursue God's will.

14a. True or false: No matter how unpleasant the thought of change may seem, it is important to know whether or not you have chosen your life's purpose.
False

14b. Discussion question: How do you deal with change, even if it is unpleasant?
Discussion question

14c. _____ with effort and time will you see God's will for your life come to pass.
Only

15. You will never have another today. You have to spend every day moving in the direction that God wants your life to go. It can feel a little threatening to get out of a routine and do something new, especially if we have been doing the same thing for a long time, but you have to be willing to get out of your comfort zone in order to find God's purpose for your life. I promise, knowing the joy of being in the center of God's will makes it all worthwhile.

15a. How often do you have to move in the direction God wants you to go?
Every day

15b. What does Andrew promise?
That it's worthwhile to know the joy of being in the center of God's will

16. There are certain people who would never hear me preach the Gospel. You have a sphere of influence—people in your life—that might never receive the full anointing God has for them unless you reach your potential. You will be happier and a much greater blessing to the people in your life once you find your purpose and start heading in that direction. God calls more people into business and labor than He calls into full-time ministry. Regardless of what you are called to do, God wants you to reach people and manifest His power in the world.

16a. What two things will you be once you find your purpose and start heading in that direction?
   A. Warm and filled from good home cooking
   B. Happier and a greater blessing to the people in your life
   C. Popular and uncontested in everything you do
   D. All of the above
   E. None of the above
   B. Happier and a greater blessing to the people in your life

16b. Discussion question: Why do you think God calls more people into business and labor than He calls into full-time ministry?
Discussion question

17. I think it would be terrible to live your whole life and not know for sure that you are doing what God created you to do. It would terrify me to go to bed and wake up not having a clue if I am following God's will. The only thing worse than not knowing God's will is knowing His will and choosing not to do it—either because you have talked yourself out of it or have let others talk you out of it. To know that God made you for a purpose and to feel unqualified or incapable of fulfilling it, is worse than not knowing at all. A God-given purpose and a life driven by the Holy Spirit motivate me to work through life's hardships. Going to work because it beats starving to death is a terrible way to live your life. You need to live your life on purpose. God has a perfect plan for your life, and His plan is better than your plan for yourself.

17a. What's the only thing worse than not knowing God's will?
Knowing His will and choosing not to do it

17b. What motivates Andrew to work through life's hardships?
    A. A God-given purpose and a life driven by the Holy Spirit
    B. Fear of failure and embarrassment
    C. Knowing he needs to keep ministering to pay the bills
    D. Pressure from what everyone expects of him
    E. A promise he made to himself a long time ago
    A. A God-given purpose and a life driven by the Holy Spirit

17c. True or false: Going to work because it beats starving to death is an awesome way to live your life.
False

17d. Discussion question: Why do you think God has the perfect plan for your life that is better than your own?
Discussion question

37. Discussion question: What do you think about the fact that God had a plan and purpose for you before you were born?

_____

_____

_____

38. Too many people are trying to figure out what to do with their lives by looking at what?
    A. The new charismatic televangelist
    B. What they see other people doing
    C. Circumstances working out a certain way
    D. Their natural abilities or a personality test
    E. The money in their bank accounts

39. Why aren't the results of a personality test true forever?

_____

_____

_____

40. True or false: Personality tests can't tell you God's real plan and purpose for your life.

41. Discussion question: Why do you think God will always call you to do something that is beyond your natural ability, forcing you to rely on Him?

_____

_____

_____

42. If you only do what you feel you are naturally equipped to do—what you are capable of doing in your own strength and ability—then you will be tempted to give _____ the credit for success.

43. True or false: No matter how unpleasant the thought of change may seem, it is important to know whether or not you have chosen your life's purpose.

44. Discussion question: How do you deal with change, even if it is unpleasant?

_____

_____

_____

45. _____ with effort and time will you see God's will for your life come to pass.

46. How often do you have to move in the direction God wants you to go?

_____

_____

_____

47. What does Andrew promise?

_____

_____

_____

48. What two things will you be once you find your purpose and start heading in that direction?
    A. Warm and filled from good home cooking
    B. Happier and a greater blessing to the people in your life
    C. Popular and uncontested in everything you do
    D. All of the above
    E. None of the above

49. Discussion question: Why do you think God calls more people into business and labor than He calls into full-time ministry?

_____

_____

_____

50. What's the only thing worse than not knowing God's will?

_____

_____

_____

51. What motivates Andrew to work through life's hardships?
    A. A God-given purpose and a life driven by the Holy Spirit
    B. Fear of failure and embarrassment
    C. Knowing he needs to keep ministering to pay the bills
    D. Pressure from what everyone expects of him
    E. A promise he made to himself a long time ago

52. True or false: Going to work because it beats starving to death is an awesome way to live your life.

53. Discussion question: Why do you think God has the perfect plan for your life that is better than your own?

_____

_____

_____

37. *Discussion question*

38. D. Their natural abilities or a personality test

39. Because they only give you a snapshot of where you are at the time you take the test

40. True

41. *Discussion question*

42. Yourself

43. False

44. *Discussion question*

45. Only

46. Every day

47. That it's worthwhile to know the joy of being in the center of God's will

48. B. Happier and a greater blessing to the people in your life

49. *Discussion question*

50. Knowing His will and choosing not to do it

51. A. A God-given purpose and a life driven by the Holy Spirit

52. False

53. *Discussion question*

GALATIANS 1:13-15

For ye have heard of my conversation in time past in the Jews' religion, how that beyond measure I persecuted the church of God, and wasted it: [14] And profited in the Jews' religion above many my equals in mine own nation, being more exceedingly zealous of the traditions of my fathers. [15] But when it pleased God, who separated me from my mother's womb, and called me by his grace.

LESSON 1.4

Ican tell you emphatically what God's primary will for your life is: to know Jesus. He is not willing that anyone should perish, but that all should come to repentance (2 Pet. 3:9). God's will for every person on earth is to know Him. It doesn't matter what you have done in the past. Paul said he was the greatest sinner of all, yet God chose him to show that anybody who calls upon the name of the Lord will be saved (Rom. 10:13). In order to be saved, or to be in right relationship with God, you must be born again.

> *Jesus answered and said unto him, Verily, verily, I say unto thee, Except a man be born again, he cannot see the kingdom of God.*
>
> JOHN 3:3

You have to be certain you are born again. A lot of churchgoers in America think that merely believing that God exists is enough to be saved, but the Bible says, *"Thou believest that there is one God; thou doest well: the devils also believe, and tremble"* (James 2:19). In other words, it's no great accomplishment to believe in God—even the devil knows that God is real. You have to do more than mentally acknowledge God's existence; you have to submit yourself to Him. You have to commit your life to Him personally, and when you do that, the Bible says you are born again from above. You get changed on the inside.

If you are already born again, great; I'm not trying to talk you out of it. But if you have not committed your life to God personally, you need to. This is the first and most important step in finding God's will for your life. You need to be certain that you have done it. A lot of people think *Well, I'm a good person. I go to church*, but that isn't enough. Sitting in a church isn't going to make you a Christian any more than sitting in a garage is going to make you a car. You must be born again.

It doesn't matter how good of a person you are. Everyone falls short of God's standard of perfection. You can't save yourself, and that's why God became a man—Jesus—and paid the price for sin on your behalf. Nothing you can do will make you worthy of receiving God's love. No amount of good works will earn you the privilege of being righteous in God's eyes. The only thing that will restore you to a right relationship with God is putting your faith in Jesus and submitting to Him as Lord of your life.

Imagine standing before God and hearing Him ask, "What makes you worthy to enter into heaven?" How would you answer? If your first thought is to tell God what a good person you are, how you read your Bible, or that your parents used to take you to church, then you aren't born again. The only correct answer is to say, "I put my faith in Jesus Christ."

The sacrifice of Jesus Christ is what makes us right with God. In order to receive His free gift of salvation, all you have to do is believe. It's so simple that people usually think it can't be that easy. But it really is that simple. Nothing is required aside from believing in the finished work of Jesus. Scripture says,

> *If thou shalt confess with thy mouth the Lord Jesus, and shalt believe in thine heart that God hath raised him from the dead, thou shalt be saved.*
>
> ROMANS 10:9

The words are easy to say, but you also have to believe what you say in your heart. You have to really mean that you are turning your life over to Jesus—which isn't to say that you'll never sin again. No one is perfect, and there are times when you fail. You have to be willing to turn the direction of your life over to the Lord and accept salvation solely on the basis of what Jesus has done for you.

Jesus has already paid for your sins, so salvation is simply a matter of receiving what God desires to give you—it's not a matter of trying to convince God to give you something He really doesn't want to. Salvation is simple, but it didn't come cheap. Jesus paid for salvation by taking the punishment you deserved in His own body on the cross. He suffered, died, and defeated death by rising again. Jesus earned salvation for you because you couldn't. So, all you have to do to be saved is say this prayer out loud, believe it in your heart, and you will be born again. It's that simple.

Father, I'm sorry for my sins. I believe Jesus died to forgive my sin, and I receive that forgiveness. Jesus, I make You my Lord. I believe that You are alive and that You now live in me. I am saved. I am forgiven. Thank You, Jesus!

God Isn't Keeping His Will a Secret

Salvation through faith in Jesus is God's universal will for every person on earth. It brings you into a personal relationship with God. It's the absolute first step in finding God's will for your life. Once you are in relationship with God, you can move on to find out what His *particular* will for your life is. God made you for one specific purpose, and your only chance of reaching your full potential is to find that purpose.

Fortunately, God wants you to know and live out His will even more than you do. He desires to reveal His will to you. For the remainder of this study guide, I will share things that you can do to draw on the power of God and cause Him to reveal His will to you.

The first thing you need to do is refuse to go any further without knowing God's will for your life. As long as you can live without knowing God's purpose for your life, you will. After you insist on finding His will and commit to seeking the Lord with your whole heart, He will immediately put everything in motion to reveal Himself to you—but the first step is making a commitment.

> *For the which cause I also suffer these things: nevertheless I am not ashamed:*
> *for I know whom I have believed, and am persuaded that he is able to keep that*
> *which I have committed unto him against that day.*
>
> 2 TIMOTHY 1:12

God is faithful and just to keep *that which we commit*. No committing, no keeping. You have to commit to something. Are you going to continue to go through life thinking, *Que sera, sera. Whatever will be, will be*? Or are you going to make a commitment to find God's will for your life? If you are willing to make a total commitment to seeking God and finding His perfect will for your life, then I would like to pray with you. This prayer will be a step of faith that is going to start the process of God revealing His will to you:

Father, I love You. I thank You for the knowledge that You desire to reveal Your will to me. I don't want to do things on my own anymore. Father, I want to know Your will. I want to know what You created me for. I want to take everything that I am and use it to accomplish Your purpose for me.

I know it's a process, but I am making a commitment to begin seeking and continue seeking, until I find. I'm not going to be content with living my life for myself. I now humble myself to You, Lord, and ask You to reveal Your will to me. Father, give me supernatural revelation.

Lord, I believe that right now the process has begun. I have made a commitment, and I believe You are going to keep that which I commit. I believe You are going to draw me to a place where I will emphatically know what Your purpose and will for my life is. I thank You, Father, in advance, knowing that You will reveal Yourself to me in a way that I can see and understand. I thank You for this in the name of Jesus. Amen.

XVIII. I can tell you emphatically what God's primary will for your life is: to know Jesus.

    A. In order to be saved, or to be in right relationship with God, you must be born again.

Jesus answered and said unto him, Verily, verily, I say unto thee, Except a man be born again, he cannot see the kingdom of God.

JOHN 3:3

    B. You have to do more than mentally acknowledge God's existence; you have to submit yourself to Him.

    C. You have to commit your life to Him personally, and when you do that, the Bible says you are born again from above—you get changed on the inside.

    D. If you have not committed your life to God personally, you need to.

    E. This is the first and most important step in finding God's will for your life.

XIX. It doesn't matter how good of a person you are—everyone falls short of God's standard of perfection.

    A. Nothing you can do will make you worthy of receiving God's love.

    B. No amount of good works will earn you the privilege of being righteous in God's eyes.

    C. The only thing that will restore you to a right relationship with God is putting your faith in Jesus and submitting to Him as Lord of your life.

If thou shalt confess with thy mouth the Lord Jesus, and shalt believe in thine heart that God hath raised him from the dead, thou shalt be saved.

ROMANS 10:9

    D. The words are easy to say, but you also have to believe what you say in your heart.

    E. You have to really mean that you are turning your life over to Jesus—which isn't to say that you'll never sin again.

    F. Jesus paid for salvation by taking the punishment you deserved in His own body on the cross.

    G. He suffered, died, and defeated death by rising again.

    H. Jesus earned salvation for you because you couldn't.

    I. So, all you have to do to be saved is say this prayer out loud, believe it in your heart, and you will be born again—it's that simple:

Father, I'm sorry for my sins. I believe Jesus died to forgive my sin, and I receive that forgiveness. Jesus, I make You my Lord. I believe that You are alive and that You now live in me. I am saved. I am forgiven. Thank You, Jesus!

XX. Once you are in relationship with God, you can move on to find out what His *particular* will for your life is.

    A. Fortunately, God wants you to know and live out His will even more than you do.

    B. For the remainder of this study guide, I will share things that you can do to draw on the power of God and cause Him to reveal His will to you.

    C. The first thing you need to do is refuse to go any further without knowing God's will for your life.

    D. As long as you can live without knowing God's purpose for your life, you will.

XXI. After you insist on finding God's will and commit to seeking Him with your whole heart, He will immediately put everything in motion to reveal Himself to you—but the first step is making a commitment.

    A. God is faithful and just to keep *that which you commit*—no committing, no keeping (2 Tim. 1:12).

    B. If you are willing to make a total commitment to seeking God and finding His perfect will for your life, then I would like to pray with you.

    C. This prayer will be a step of faith that is going to start the process of God revealing His will to you:

    Father, I love You. I thank You for the knowledge that You desire to reveal Your will to me. I don't want to do things on my own anymore. Father, I want to know Your will. I want to know what You created me for. I want to take everything that I am and use it to accomplish Your purpose for me.

    I know it's a process, but I am making a commitment to begin seeking and continue seeking, until I find. I'm not going to be content with living my life for myself. I now humble myself to You, Lord, and ask You to reveal Your will to me. Father, give me supernatural revelation.

    Lord, I believe that right now the process has begun. I have made a commitment, and I believe You are going to keep that which I commit. I believe You are going to draw me to a place where I will emphatically know what Your purpose and will for my life is. I thank You, Father, in advance, knowing that You will reveal Yourself to me in a way that I can see and understand. I thank You for this in the name of Jesus. Amen.

18. I can tell you emphatically what God's primary will for your life is: to know Jesus. In order to be saved, or to be in right relationship with God, you must be born again.

> *Jesus answered and said unto him, Verily, verily, I say unto thee, Except a man be born again, he cannot see the kingdom of God.*
>
> JOHN 3:3

You have to do more than mentally acknowledge God's existence; you have to submit yourself to Him. You have to commit your life to Him personally, and when you do that, the Bible says you are born again from above—you get changed on the inside. If you have not committed your life to God personally, you need to. This is the first and most important step in finding God's will for your life.

18a.   What is God's primary will for your life?
To know Jesus

18b.   Read John 3:3. What happens when you commit your life to God personally?
The Bible says you are born again from above—you get changed on the inside

18c.   If you haven't committed your life to God, what do you need to do?
    A.   Ask God if it's His will that you do so
    B.   Wait until the next altar call
    C.   Commit your life to God
    D.   All of the above
    E.   None of the above
    C.   Commit your life to God

19. It doesn't matter how good of a person you are—everyone falls short of God's standard of perfection. Nothing you can do will make you worthy of receiving God's love. No amount of good works will earn you the privilege of being righteous in God's eyes. The only thing that will restore you to a right relationship with God is putting your faith in Jesus and submitting to Him as Lord of your life.

> *If thou shalt confess with thy mouth the Lord Jesus, and shalt believe in thine heart that God hath raised him from the dead, thou shalt be saved.*
>
> ROMANS 10:9

The words are easy to say, but you also have to believe what you say in your heart. You have to really mean that you are turning your life over to Jesus—which isn't to say that you'll never sin again. Jesus paid for salvation by taking the punishment you deserved in His own body on the cross. He suffered, died, and defeated death by rising again. Jesus earned salvation for you because you couldn't. So, all you have to do to be saved is say this prayer out loud, believe it in your heart, and you will be born again—it's that simple:

> *Father, I'm sorry for my sins. I believe Jesus died to forgive my sin, and I receive that forgiveness. Jesus, I make You my Lord. I believe that You are alive and that You now live in me. I am saved. I am forgiven. Thank You, Jesus!*

19a. True or false: There is something you can do to make you worthy of receiving God's love.
    False

19b. True or false: No amount of good works will earn you the privilege of being righteous in God's eyes.
    True

19c. What is the only thing that will restore you to a right relationship with God?
    Putting your faith in Jesus and submitting to Him as Lord of your life

19d. Discussion question: Read Romans 10:9. Why do you think you have to believe in your heart?
    Discussion question

19e. How did Jesus pay for salvation?
    A. With all the gold He received from the wise men
    B. With the gold that Peter retrieved from the fish's mouth
    C. With the money He'd saved from His carpentry work
    D. With the condition that He would make you pay for it at a later time
    E. By taking the punishment you deserved in His own body on the cross
    E. By taking the punishment you deserved in His own body on the cross

20. Once you are in relationship with God, you can move on to find out what His *particular* will for your life is. Fortunately, God wants you to know and live out His will even more than you do. For the remainder of this study guide, I will share things that you can do to draw on the power of God and cause Him to reveal His will to you. The first thing you need to do is refuse to go any further without knowing God's will for your life. As long as you can live without knowing God's purpose for your life, you will.

20a. Once you are in relationship with God, what can you do next?
You can move on to find out what His particular will for your life is

20b. Discussion question: Why is it good news that God wants you to know and live out His will even more than you do?
Discussion question

20c. If you can live without knowing God's purposes for your life, what will you do?
You'll live without knowing God's purposes for your life

21. After you insist on finding God's will and commit to seeking Him with your whole heart, He will immediately put everything in motion to reveal Himself to you—but the first step is making a commitment. God is faithful and just to keep *that which you commit*—no committing, no keeping (2 Tim. 1:12). If you are willing to make a total commitment to seeking God and finding His perfect will for your life, then I would like to pray with you. This prayer will be a step of faith that is going to start the process of God revealing His will to you:

> *Father, I love You. I thank You for the knowledge that You desire to reveal Your will to me. I don't want to do things on my own anymore. Father, I want to know Your will. I want to know what You created me for. I want to take everything that I am and use it to accomplish Your purpose for me.*
>
> *I know it's a process, but I am making a commitment to begin seeking and continue seeking, until I find. I'm not going to be content with living my life for myself. I now humble myself to You, Lord, and ask You to reveal Your will to me. Father, give me supernatural revelation.*
>
> *Lord, I believe that right now the process has begun. I have made a commitment, and I believe You are going to keep that which I commit. I believe You are going to draw me to a place where I will emphatically know what Your purpose and will for my life is. I thank You, Father, in advance, knowing that You will reveal Yourself to me in a way that I can see and understand. I thank You for this in the name of Jesus. Amen.*

21a. After you insist on finding His will and commit to seeking the Lord with your whole heart, what will He do?
    A. Nothing
    B. Say thank you
    C. Relent from punishing you for the day
    D. All of the above
    E. None of the above
    E. None of the above

21b. According to 2 Timothy 1:12, what will God keep?
    Only what you commit to Him

54. What is God's primary will for your life?

_____

_____

_____

55. Read John 3:3. What happens when you commit your life to God personally?

_____

_____

_____

56. If you haven't committed your life to God, what do you need to do?
    A. Ask God if it's His will that you do so
    B. Wait until the next altar call
    C. Commit your life to God
    D. All of the above
    E. None of the above

57. True or false: There is something you can do to make you worthy of receiving God's love.

58. True or false: No amount of good works will earn you the privilege of being righteous in God's eyes.

59. What is the only thing that will restore you to a right relationship with God?

_____

_____

_____

60. Discussion question: Read Romans 10:9. Why do you think you have to believe in your heart?

_____

_____

_____

61. How did Jesus pay for salvation?
    A. With all the gold He received from the wise men
    B. With the gold that Peter retrieved from the fish's mouth
    C. With the money He'd saved from His carpentry work
    D. With the condition that He would make you pay for it at a later time
    E. By taking the punishment you deserved in His own body on the cross

62. Once you are in relationship with God, what can you do next?

_____

_____

_____

63. Discussion question: Why is it good news that God wants you to know and live out His will even more than you do?

_____

_____

_____

64. If you can live without knowing God's purposes for your life, what will you do?

_____

_____

_____

65. After you insist on finding His will and commit to seeking the Lord with your whole heart, what will He do?
    A. Nothing
    B. Say thank you
    C. Relent from punishing you for the day
    D. All of the above
    E. None of the above

66. According to 2 Timothy 1:12, what will God keep?

_____

_____

_____

54. To know Jesus

55. The Bible says you are born again from above—you get changed on the inside

56. C. Commit your life to God

57. False

58. True

59. Putting your faith in Jesus and submitting to Him as Lord of your life

60. *Discussion question*

61. E. By taking the punishment you deserved in His own body on the cross

62. You can move on to find out what His particular will for your life is

63. *Discussion question*

64. You'll live without knowing God's purposes for your life

65. E. None of the above

66. Only what you commit to Him

2 PETER 3:9

The Lord is not slack concerning his promise, as some men count slackness; but is longsuffering to us-ward, not willing that any should perish, but that all should come to repentance.

ROMANS 10:13

For whosoever shall call upon the name of the Lord shall be saved.

JOHN 3:3

Jesus answered and said unto him, Verily, verily, I say unto thee, Except a man be born again, he cannot see the kingdom of God.

JAMES 2:19

Thou believest that there is one God; thou doest well: the devils also believe, and tremble.

ROMANS 10:9

That if thou shalt confess with thy mouth the Lord Jesus, and shalt believe in thine heart that God hath raised him from the dead, thou shalt be saved.

2 TIMOTHY 1:12

For the which cause I also suffer these things: nevertheless I am not ashamed: for I know whom I have believed, and am persuaded that he is able to keep that which I have committed unto him against that day.

GOD OF SECOND CHANCES

LESSON 2.1

Our lives can get so complicated that it's hard to figure out how to get from where we are to where God wants us to be. We all make mistakes, and it's easy to start thinking about what might have been if we had done just a few things differently. But I don't think it's helpful to regret things we have done and start asking ourselves, "What if I would have followed God? What if I hadn't done this or that?" Satan uses thoughts like that to beat us up. Rather than reliving the past, it's better to understand that God has ways of getting us from where we are to where we need to be—after we surrender our lives to Him. It's always better for us to focus on the solution instead of the problem.

The Old Testament book of 1 Samuel tells the story of Saul, Israel's first king. Saul's story is miraculous from the beginning. He was anointed king while he was out searching for some lost livestock. Then he stopped by to ask the prophet Samuel for help. He went there thinking that Samuel might be able to tell him where his lost donkeys were, but instead, Samuel told him that he was going to be the first king of Israel (1 Sam. 9:14-10:1). At that time, however, Saul had no desire to be king.

Despite Saul's humble beginnings, he was anointed by God and became a powerful ruler. He led the nation of Israel in battle and won great victories. The people rallied around him. But two years into his reign, the Philistines gathered to fight against him in such large numbers that the men of Israel became afraid and ran off to hide in caves.

Saul regrouped the people to fight against the Philistines while he waited for Samuel to come offer a sacrifice before leading his men into battle. (The offering was a request for the Lord's blessing before they fought the enemy.) Saul waited the appointed time for Samuel to arrive, but he didn't come. The people grew restless and began to scatter. It was a crisis situation. So, Saul decided to make the burnt offering himself, instead of waiting for Samuel any longer.

And Saul said, Bring hither a burnt offering to me, and peace offerings. And he offered the burnt offering. [10] And it came to pass, that as soon as he had made an end of offering the burnt offering, behold, Samuel came; and Saul went out to meet him, that he might salute him. [11] And Samuel said, What hast thou done? And Saul said, Because I saw that the people were scattered from me, and that thou camest not within the days appointed, and that the Philistines gathered themselves together at Michmash; [12] Therefore said I, The Philistines will come down now upon me to Gilgal, and I have not made supplication unto the LORD: I forced myself therefore, and offered a burnt offering.

1 SAMUEL 13:9-12

In those days, only priests who were anointed by God could make burnt offering sacrifices. We don't know what caused Samuel's delay, but regardless, Saul was wrong in overstepping his bounds and moving into the office of a priest. Saul wasn't anointed to be *priest*; he was anointed to be *king*. By assuming the role of priest, he took authority that he knew he didn't have. Saul said *"I forced myself,"* which shows that he knew it was wrong. He was admitting that normally, he wouldn't have done such a thing but that the situation compelled him to do it. So, he did it even though he knew it was wrong.

Saul's behavior reveals a character flaw that's true of many people today—the tendency to do whatever is in their immediate best interests, regardless of whether or not it's the right thing to do. Christians shouldn't live like that. We need to be people of integrity. If God tells us to do something, we should do it. God's will should be nonnegotiable for us, regardless of the circumstances or consequences. Unfortunately, not many people live that way.

Anyone who allows an excuse to cause them to deviate from what they know is right will end up getting off course. We need to get to a place where we drive a stake in the ground and say, "This is nonnegotiable. If God tells me to do something, I'll stand here and do it, even if it kills me. I will not change." We have to be uncompromising about the will of God because we will veer off track if we start giving in to circumstances. Saul knew he wasn't supposed to offer that burnt offering, but he forced himself because it was the convenient thing to do. It might have seemed like a good reason at the time, but he knew he was disobeying God. He compromised.

And Samuel said to Saul, Thou hast done foolishly: thou hast not kept the commandment of the LORD thy God, which he commanded thee: for now would the LORD have established thy kingdom upon Israel for ever. [14] But now thy kingdom shall not continue: the LORD hath sought him a man after his own heart, and the LORD hath commanded him to be captain over his people, because thou hast not kept that which the LORD commanded thee.

1 SAMUEL 13:13-14

This is amazing. Samuel said that if Saul had obeyed God that day, he would have ruled over Israel *forever*. Instead, God chose David to replace Saul as king. If Saul had obeyed God, there never would have been a King David. We never would have heard of him, because David wasn't God's first choice. Saul was *not* just a temporary king until David came along. Saul was God's first choice.

This incident happened in the second year of Saul's reign (1 Sam. 13:1). Then Saul reigned for another thirty-eight years (Acts 13:21). We also know that David was thirty years old when he finally became king at the end of Saul's reign (2 Sam. 5:4). So, that means that Samuel prophesied that "the Lord has sought a man after His own heart" eight years before David was even born! God said He had sought out a man after his own heart, long before David was even conceived.

David was born to be king—that was his purpose—but he wasn't God's first choice. David became king because Saul failed to do what God called him to do. But look at what God did with second best! David became a mighty man of God. He was a man after God's own heart. And he accomplished great things.

You shouldn't speculate about what could have or should have been in your life. If you have wasted time chasing your own dreams or if you made some bad decisions, don't get caught up in mulling over the past. Just start seeking God. Submit yourself to God. He can take you from wherever you are today and make His *plan B* for your life better than you could ever have imagined *plan A* would be. The fastest route to God's perfect will for your life is to simply start seeking Him today.

Saul's life also demonstrates that God doesn't sovereignly move you around and make everything automatically work out according to His will. Saul didn't cooperate with God; therefore, he missed God's will for his life. Don't get worried, though—God has never had anybody qualified working for Him yet! You will make mistakes. But God is so awesome that He can take the little bit you submit to Him and use it to accomplish His will.

OUTLINE • 2.1

I. Our lives can get so complicated that it's hard to figure out how to get from where we are to where God wants us to be.

    A. We all make mistakes, and it's easy to start thinking about what might have been if we had done just a few things differently.

    B. Rather than reliving the past, it's better to understand that God has ways of getting us from where we are to where we need to be—after we surrender our lives to Him.

    C. It's always better for us to focus on the solution instead of the problem.

II. First Samuel tells the story of Saul, Israel's first king.

    A. Saul had no desire to be king, but he was anointed by God and became a powerful ruler with the support of the people.

    B. But two years into his reign, he decided to make the burnt offering that Samuel was supposed to make, because Samuel hadn't shown (the offering was a request for the Lord's blessing before they fought the enemy).

And Saul said, Bring hither a burnt offering to me, and peace offerings. And he offered the burnt offering. [10] And it came to pass, that as soon as he had made an end of offering the burnt offering, behold, Samuel came; and Saul went out to meet him, that he might salute him. [11] And Samuel said, What hast thou done? And Saul said, Because I saw that the people were scattered from me, and that thou camest not within the days appointed, and that the Philistines gathered themselves together at Michmash; [12] Therefore said I, The Philistines will come down now upon me to Gilgal, and I have not made supplication unto the LORD: I forced myself therefore, and offered a burnt offering.

1 SAMUEL 13:9-12

    C. In those days, only priests who were anointed by God could make burnt offering sacrifices.

    D. Regardless of what delayed Samuel, Saul was wrong in overstepping his bounds and moving into the office of a priest.

    E. Saul said *"I forced myself,"* which shows that he knew it was wrong.

    F. He admitted that normally he wouldn't have done such a thing but that the situation compelled him to do it.

III. Saul's behavior reveals a character flaw that's true of many people today—the tendency to do whatever is in their immediate best interests, regardless of whether or not it's the right thing to do.

    A. We need to get to a place where we say, "This is nonnegotiable. If God tells me to do something, I'll stand here and do it, even if it kills me. I will not change."

B. We have to be uncompromising about the will of God because we will veer off track if we start giving in to circumstances.

C. Saul knew he wasn't supposed to offer that burnt offering, but he forced himself because it was the convenient thing to do—he compromised.

IV. Samuel said that if Saul had obeyed God that day, he would have ruled over Israel *forever* (1 Sam. 13:13-14).

A. If Saul had obeyed God, there never would have been a King David.

B. Saul was *not* just a temporary king until David came along; he was God's first choice.

C. David became king because Saul failed to do what God called him to do, but look at what God did with second best!

    i. David became a mighty man of God.

    ii. He was a man after God's own heart.

    iii. He accomplished great things.

V. You shouldn't speculate about what could have or should have been in your life.

A. If you have wasted time chasing your own dreams or if you made some bad decisions, don't get caught up in mulling over the past—just start seeking God and submit to Him.

B. He can take you from wherever you are today and make His *plan B* for your life better than you could ever have imagined *plan A* would be.

C. The fastest route to God's perfect will for your life is to simply start seeking Him today.

VI. Saul's life also demonstrates that God doesn't sovereignly move you around and make everything automatically work out according to His will.

A. Saul didn't cooperate with God; therefore, he missed God's will for his life.

B. Don't get worried, though—God has never had anybody qualified working for Him yet!

C. You will make mistakes, but God is so awesome that He can take the little bit you submit to Him and use it to accomplish His will.

TEACHER'S GUIDE • 2.1

1. Our lives can get so complicated that it's hard to figure out how to get from where we are to where God wants us to be. We all make mistakes, and it's easy to start thinking about what might have been if we had done just a few things differently. Rather than reliving the past, it's better to understand that God has ways of getting us from where we are to where we need to be—after we surrender our lives to Him. It's always better for us to focus on the solution instead of the problem.

1a.   It's better to understand that God has ways of getting you from where you are to where you need to be—after what?
After you surrender your life to Him

1b.   What is always better to focus on?
A.   What others think about you
B.   The next time to eat
C.   The solution instead of the problem
D.   All of the above
E.   None of the above
C.   The solution instead of the problem

2. First Samuel tells the story of Saul, Israel's first king. Saul had no desire to be king, but he was anointed by God and became a powerful ruler with the support of the people. But two years into his reign, he decided to make the burnt offering that Samuel was supposed to make, because Samuel hadn't shown (the offering was a request for the Lord's blessing before they fought the enemy).

> *And Saul said, Bring hither a burnt offering to me, and peace offerings. And he offered the burnt offering. [10] And it came to pass, that as soon as he had made an end of offering the burnt offering, behold, Samuel came; and Saul went out to meet him, that he might salute him. [11] And Samuel said, What hast thou done? And Saul said, Because I saw that the people were scattered from me, and that thou camest not within the days appointed, and that the Philistines gathered themselves together at Michmash; [12] Therefore said I, The Philistines will come down now upon me to Gilgal, and I have not made supplication unto the Lord: I forced myself therefore, and offered a burnt offering.*
> 1 SAMUEL 13:9-12

In those days, only priests who were anointed by God could make burnt offering sacrifices. Regardless of what delayed Samuel, Saul was wrong in overstepping his bounds and moving into the office of a priest. Saul said *"I forced myself,"* which shows that he knew it was wrong. He admitted that normally he wouldn't have done such a thing but that the situation compelled him to do it.

2a.   Discussion question: Read 1 Samuel 13:9-12. If you were in a situation where you had waited a specified time for something, would you have done the same thing King Saul did?
Discussion question

3. Saul's behavior reveals a character flaw that's true of many people today—the tendency to do whatever is in their immediate best interests, regardless of whether or not it's the right thing to do. We need to get to a place where we say, "This is nonnegotiable. If God tells me to do something, I'll stand here and do it, even if it kills me. I will not change." We have to be uncompromising about the will of God because we will veer off track if we start giving in to circumstances. Saul knew he wasn't supposed to offer that burnt offering, but he forced himself because it was the convenient thing to do—he compromised.

3a.   What does Saul's behavior reveal?
       A character flaw that's true of many people today—the tendency to do whatever is in their immediate best interests, regardless of whether or not it's the right thing to do

3b.   True or false: You need to get to a place where you say, "This is nonnegotiable. If God tells me to do something, I'll stand here and do it, even if it kills me. I will not change."
       True

4. Samuel said that if Saul had obeyed God that day, he would have ruled over Israel *forever* (1 Sam. 13:13-14). If Saul had obeyed God, there never would have been a King David. Saul was *not* just a temporary king until David came along; he was God's first choice. David became king because Saul failed to do what God called him to do, but look at what God did with second best! David became a mighty man of God. He was a man after God's own heart. He accomplished great things.

4a.   Discussion question: What do you think about the idea that there never would have been a King David if Saul had obeyed?
       Discussion question

4b.   What did God accomplish through David, His second best?
       David became a mighty man of God, he was a man after God's own heart, and he accomplished great things

5. You shouldn't speculate about what could have or should have been in your life. If you have wasted time chasing your own dreams or if you made some bad decisions, don't get caught up in mulling over the past—just start seeking God and submit to Him. He can take you from wherever you are today and make His *plan B* for your life better than you could ever have imagined *plan A* would be. The fastest route to God's perfect will for your life is to simply start seeking Him today.

5a.   What shouldn't you speculate about?
    A. Who the greatest in the kingdom of God is
    B. What could have or should have been in your life
    C. Where to invest your money
    D. Whether you should've eaten that last slice of pizza last night
    E. Who's going to win the next ball game
    B. What could have or should have been in your life

5b.   What should you do instead?
    Start seeking God and submit to Him

5c.   True or false: This is not the fastest route to God's perfect will for your life.
    False

6. Saul's life also demonstrates that God doesn't sovereignly move you around and make everything automatically work out according to His will. Saul didn't cooperate with God; therefore, he missed God's will for his life. Don't get worried, though—God has never had anybody qualified working for Him yet! You will make mistakes, but God is so awesome that He can take the little bit you submit to Him and use it to accomplish His will.

6a.   How do you know that Saul's life demonstrates that God doesn't sovereignly move you around and make everything automatically work out according to His will?
    Because Saul didn't cooperate with God

6b.   True or false: God has people who are qualified working for Him.
    False

6c.   Discussion question: How do you think God can take the little bit you submit to Him and use it to accomplish His will?
    Discussion question

DISCIPLESHIP QUESTIONS • 2.1

1. It's better to understand that God has ways of getting you from where you are to where you need to be—after what?

_____

_____

_____

2. What is always better to focus on?
   A. What others think about you
   B. The next time to eat
   C. The solution instead of the problem
   D. All of the above
   E. None of the above

3. Discussion question: Read 1 Samuel 13:9-12. If you were in a situation where you had waited a specified time for something, would you have done the same thing King Saul did?

_____

_____

_____

4. What does Saul's behavior reveal?

_____

_____

_____

5. True or false: You need to get to a place where you say, "This is nonnegotiable. If God tells me to do something, I'll stand here and do it, even if it kills me. I will not change."

6. Discussion question: What do you think about the idea that there never would have been a King David if Saul had obeyed?

_____

_____

_____

7. What did God accomplish through David, His second best?

_____

_____

_____

8. What shouldn't you speculate about?
   A. Who the greatest in the kingdom of God is
   B. What could have or should have been in your life
   C. Where to invest your money
   D. Whether you should've eaten that last slice of pizza last night
   E. Who's going to win the next ball game

9. What should you do instead?

_____

_____

_____

10. True or false: This is not the fastest route to God's perfect will for your life.

11. How do you know that Saul's life demonstrates that God doesn't sovereignly move you around and make everything automatically work out according to His will?

_____

_____

_____

12. True or false: God has people who are qualified working for Him.

13. Discussion question: How do you think God can take the little bit you submit to Him and use it to accomplish His will?

_____

_____

_____

ANSWER KEY • 2.1

1. After you surrender your life to Him
2. C. The solution instead of the problem
3. *Discussion question*
4. A character flaw that's true of many people today—the tendency to do whatever is in their immediate best interests, regardless of whether or not it's the right thing to do
5. True
6. *Discussion question*
7. David became a mighty man of God, he was a man after God's own heart, and he accomplished great things
8. B. What could have or should have been in your life
9. Start seeking God and submit to Him
10. False
11. Because Saul didn't cooperate with God
12. False
13. *Discussion question*

1 SAMUEL 9:14-10:1

And they went up into the city: and when they were come into the city, behold, Samuel came out against them, for to go up to the high place. [15] Now the LORD had told Samuel in his ear a day before Saul came, saying, [16] To morrow about this time I will send thee a man out of the land of Benjamin, and thou shalt anoint him to be captain over my people Israel, that he may save my people out of the hand of the Philistines: for I have looked upon my people, because their cry is come unto me. [17] And when Samuel saw Saul, the LORD said unto him, Behold the man whom I spake to thee of! this same shall reign over my people. [18] Then Saul drew near to Samuel in the gate, and said, Tell me, I pray thee, where the seer's house is. [19] And Samuel answered Saul, and said, I am the seer: go up before me unto the high place; for ye shall eat with me to day, and to morrow I will let thee go, and will tell thee all that is in thine heart. [20] And as for thine asses that were lost three days ago, set not thy mind on them; for they are found. And on whom is all the desire of Israel? Is it not on thee, and on all thy father's house? [21] And Saul answered and said, Am not I a Benjamite, of the smallest of the tribes of Israel? and my family the least of all the families of the tribe of Benjamin? wherefore then speakest thou so to me? [22] And Samuel took Saul and his servant, and brought them into the parlour, and made them sit in the chiefest place among them that were bidden, which were about thirty persons. [23] And Samuel said unto the cook, Bring the portion which I gave thee, of which I said unto thee, Set it by thee. [24] And the cook took up the shoulder, and that which was upon it, and set it before Saul. And Samuel said, Behold that which is left! set it before thee, and eat: for unto this time hath it been kept for thee since I said, I have invited the people. So Saul did eat with Samuel that day. [25] And when they were come down from the high place into the city, Samuel communed with Saul upon the top of the house. [26] And they arose early: and it came to pass about the spring of the day, that Samuel called Saul to the top of the house, saying, Up, that I may send thee away. And Saul arose, and they went out both of them, he and Samuel, abroad. [27] And as they were going down to the end of the city, Samuel said to Saul, Bid the servant pass on before us, (and he passed on,) but stand thou still a while, that I may shew thee the word of God. [10:1] Then Samuel took a vial of oil, and poured it upon his head, and kissed him, and said, Is it not because the LORD hath anointed thee to be captain over his inheritance?

1 SAMUEL 13:9-14

And Saul said, Bring hither a burnt offering to me, and peace offerings. And he offered the burnt offering. [10] And it came to pass, that as soon as he had made an end of offering the burnt offering, behold, Samuel came; and Saul went out to meet him, that he might salute him. [11] And Samuel said, What hast thou done? And Saul said, Because I saw that the people were scattered from me, and that thou camest not within the days appointed, and that the Philistines gathered themselves together at Michmash; [12] Therefore said I, The Philistines will come down now upon me to Gilgal, and I have not made supplication unto the Lord: I forced myself therefore, and offered a burnt offering. [13] And Samuel said to Saul, Thou hast done foolishly: thou hast not kept the commandment of the Lord thy God, which he commanded thee: for now would the Lord have established thy kingdom upon Israel for ever. [14] But now thy kingdom shall not continue: the Lord hath sought him a man after his own heart, and the Lord hath commanded him to be captain over his people, because thou hast not kept that which the Lord commanded thee.

1 SAMUEL 13:1

Saul reigned one year; and when he had reigned two years over Israel.

ACTS 13:21

And afterward they desired a king: and God gave unto them Saul the son of Cis, a man of the tribe of Benjamin, by the space of forty years.

2 SAMUEL 5:4

David was thirty years old when he began to reign, and he reigned forty years.

LESSON 2.2

And it came to pass, after the year was expired, at the time when kings go forth to battle, that David sent Joab, and his servants with him, and all Israel; and they destroyed the children of Ammon, and besieged Rabbah. But David tarried still at Jerusalem.

2 SAMUEL 11:1

David was a man after God's own heart even though he didn't do everything perfectly. In those days, kings were forced to wage war when the seasons and weather allowed. This scripture says that it was time for kings to go forth to battle. David was king, so he should have been leading his troops in battle. But David had become so prosperous that he didn't need to go; he had generals under him who could lead the troops for him. So, David stayed home and got away from what God called him to do.

When David was running for his life from Saul and it looked like he could die at any moment, he sought God with his whole heart. After he became king, he subdued his enemies, extended the borders of the nation of Israel, and prospered greatly. God blessed him, and he was more successful than any other king before him. But he stopped seeking after God wholeheartedly.

The awesome truth we need to understand here is that the greatest temptation we face in life is success. Hardship is not the worst situation in our lives. Even someone with a minimal commitment to the Lord will seek Him when the pressure is on. Failure and disaster typically drive us into the arms of God. Success is different: It makes us feel like we can make it all on our own. When everything is going good and the pressure is off, or when we don't have to seek God because it looks like everything is going our way, the contents of our hearts will be revealed. Success, not failure, is the true test of character. The question is, are we going to seek God as strongly during the good times as we do when we are struggling?

The majority of people seek the Lord more when they are in trouble. When everything is fine, they forget all about God—they don't seek Him, they don't pray, and they don't study the Word. This is what makes them more vulnerable after a victory than they are during life's struggles. When things are good, they tend to forget their need for God—which leads to trouble.

> *And it came to pass in an eveningtide, that David arose from off his bed, and walked upon the roof of the king's house: and from the roof he saw a woman washing herself; and the woman was very beautiful to look upon. [3] And David sent and enquired after the woman. And one said, Is not this Bathsheba, the daughter of Eliam, the wife of Uriah the Hittite? [4] And David sent messengers, and took her; and she came in unto him, and he lay with her; for she was purified from her uncleanness: and she returned unto her house. [5] And the woman conceived, and sent and told David, and said, I am with child.*
>
> 2 SAMUEL 11:2-5

David was bored. He was sleeping all day, staying up all night, and not doing the things God called him to do as king. If he had been out fighting his battles, this temptation would never have come. David was bored hanging around the palace and ended up getting into trouble. He committed adultery with Bathsheba, and she conceived a child. To cover up their adultery, David plotted the murder of Bathsheba's husband, Uriah—who was one of the mighty men off fighting the wars David himself should have been fighting. After Uriah was dead, David took Bathsheba as his wife (2 Sam. 11:6-26).

David got himself into a pretty bad situation, which shows how even a person who has a heart for God can get way off track. The lesson for us is that when things are going well, we should seek God even more than we have been. The moment we achieve our dreams is the time we are most vulnerable to an attack. After a victory, we need to be more dependent on God than we have ever been in our lives.

The Bible says, *"But the thing that David had done displeased the LORD"* (2 Sam. 11:27). Boy, that's putting it mildly. God was ticked off! The Lord sent the prophet Nathan to expose what David had done. Nathan went to David and told him a story about a rich man who stole his poor neighbor's only lamb, killed it, and used it to feed a guest. David said, "Any man who would do such a thing deserves to die!" After David made his pronouncement, Nathan said "You are that man" and gave a prophecy that the child conceived by Bathsheba in adultery would die (2 Sam. 12:1-14).

I'm reading between the lines here, but I believe that the reason Nathan presented the prophecy in parable form is that God was letting David prescribe his own judgment. Scripture says that God will show mercy to those who have shown mercy to others, but to those who haven't shown mercy, God will have no mercy (e.g., James 2:13 and 2 Sam. 22:26). David knew this principle because he had written about it himself. If David had been merciful, I believe he would have received mercy in return. But because he showed no mercy to the man in this parable, David passed sentence on himself and received no mercy. As a result, the child died and there was turmoil in his household.

After the death of his baby, it says that David comforted Bathsheba, and they conceived another son whom they called Solomon. The Lord loved the child and sent the prophet Nathan to announce that his name was Jedidiah (2 Sam. 12:25), which means *beloved of the Lord* in Hebrew. God anointed Solomon to be David's replacement as king of Israel (1 Kin. 1:17 and 1 Chr. 28:5), and he became so prosperous that he didn't even take any account of the silver in his kingdom (1 Kin. 10:21).

God never wanted David and Bathsheba to have a relationship. But after it was done, they repented. Then God took the second child born to them and blessed him. The Bible says that Solomon was the richest man who will ever live—not just the richest man of his day (2 Chr. 1:12). It says there will never be another man who approaches the wisdom and the riches of Solomon. God knows how to work things out for good!

All of this came to a person who was totally outside of God's original plan and purpose. Saul was God's original choice—David was second best. Then David blew it! His relationship with Bathsheba was never God's will. Yet, after they repented, God blessed their marriage. Bathsheba is the virtuous woman whom Solomon wrote about in the book of Proverbs. And Solomon was greatly blessed by God.

Maybe you think you have blown it because of bad decisions you have made in the past, but you can't blow it any more than David did. Yet God took the mess David made of his life and worked it together for good—to the extent that he is remembered as a great man. He certainly had faults and problems, but overall, David was used by God in a mighty way. We still sing about "the sure mercies of David" and recognize him as the "sweet psalmist of Israel."

God did all of this with a person who wasn't His original choice. Even when this man messed up, God worked it out for good. Four or five hundred years after David died, God was still blessing the nation of Israel. He wouldn't take His mercies away from them for the sake of His servant David. God made an everlasting covenant with David, resulting in blessings to his descendants even when they weren't serving Him. And all of this came through someone who missed it big time.

I hope this encourages you. You may have made some less-than-perfect choices, but it is pointless to spend your time regretting the past. People have come to me and said, "I'm not sure I married the right person." It doesn't do you any good to go there now; you're married, and just like David and Bathsheba, you are committed. It would be wrong to walk away or try to reverse your life and go back. You are where you are because of the choices you have made. The thing to do is humble yourself, seek God, and realize that He can take where you are right now and work everything together for good.

God's Positioning System

Regardless of what you have been through, God can take your life and make it all work out. We know that God doesn't cause the negative things in our lives, but He can still make everything turn out for good. If you have made some wrong decisions, just repent and move on. The Lord can make your life right again.

David made some serious mistakes that cost him a great deal of agony—decisions that also cost his family a lot of pain. David's daughter Tamar was raped by her brother Amnon (2 Sam. 13:10-14), and then David's son Absalom killed Amnon to avenge Tamar (2 Sam. 13:28-29). Eventually, Absalom tried to kill David and usurp the throne (2 Sam. 15:10). David had a lot of pain and turmoil in his life as a result of the poor decisions he made. He could have beaten himself up over his mistakes, but instead, he trusted God. He chose to be strong in the grace that is in the Lord (2 Tim. 2:1). This is a great lesson for all of us.

I am absolutely convinced that regardless of where you are today or how badly you may have missed God's will for your life, He still has a plan for you. The Apostle Paul wrote in his letter to the Romans,

> *For the gifts and calling of God are without repentance.*
> ROMANS 11:29

God doesn't change. Whatever His purpose for your life was when He created you hasn't changed either. You might be a long way from where God wants you to be right now, but God can get you where you need to be. Modern technology allows you to have a global positioning system (GPS) in your car to help you find your way around town.

GPS devices even speak to you and tell you where to turn. But when you are driving somewhere and make a wrong turn, the GPS doesn't freak out and say, "You missed it. You'll never get there now." No, if you make a wrong turn, the GPS says, "Recalculating." It refigures your directions and tells you what to do next in order to get where you need to go—it will still get you to your destination. Missing a turn doesn't mean you give up and go home. God is at least as good as a GPS. It doesn't matter where you are—God can recalculate. God can take what you have done and figure a way to get you back on track. You can still get where God planned for you to go.

The gifts and the calling of God never change. You may have made some wrong turns in your life, but God's will for you has not changed. He still has a plan for you. Even if you have made a royal mess of your life, God can take what you have done and cause it to work together for good. It's sort of like a master chess player who is engaged in a chess match; it doesn't matter what move his opponent makes, the master player can always use that move to his advantage. Likewise, it doesn't matter what the devil does, and it doesn't matter how much you blow it or mess up—God is able to take whatever you have done to ruin your life and turn it around.

Take Heart

I hope these biblical examples have encouraged you to take heart. God's grace is infinitely bigger than whatever you have done wrong. Your failings are no match for His grace—they aren't even worthy to mention in the same breath. You just need to humble yourself and submit your life to the Lord. Yield to Him and say, "God, here I am. Do with me what You want." God can redeem your situation. He can redeem the last days.

God hasn't given up on you. The simple fact that you are reading this study guide shows that God is drawing you and trying to reach out to you. Not a single person alive is beyond hope. No one has messed up their life so badly that God can't take it and do something supernatural with it. But you can't do things the way you always have in the past and expect different results. You're going to have to humble yourself and submit yourself to God.

OUTLINE • 2.2

VII. Second Samuel 11:1 says that it was time for kings to go forth to battle, so David should have been out leading his troops.

    A. But he stayed home and got away from what God called him to do.

    B. When David was running for his life from Saul and it looked like he could die at any moment, he sought God with his whole heart.

    C. After he became king, God blessed him and he was more successful than any other king before him, but he stopped seeking after God wholeheartedly.

    D. The awesome truth we need to understand here is that success, not failure, is the true test of character.

    E. The question is, are we going to seek God as strongly during the good times as we do when we are struggling?

VIII. When everything is fine, the majority of people tend to forget their need for God—which leads to trouble:

> *And it came to pass in an eveningtide, that David arose from off his bed, and walked upon the roof of the king's house: and from the roof he saw a woman washing herself; and the woman was very beautiful to look upon. [3] And David sent and enquired after the woman. And one said, Is not this Bathsheba, the daughter of Eliam, the wife of Uriah the Hittite? [4] And David sent messengers, and took her; and she came in unto him, and he lay with her; for she was purified from her uncleanness: and she returned unto her house. [5] And the woman conceived, and sent and told David, and said, I am with child.*
>
> 2 SAMUEL 11:2-5

    A. If David had been doing what God called him to do as king, this temptation would never have come.

    B. To cover up their adultery, David plotted the murder of Bathsheba's husband, Uriah—who was one of the mighty men off fighting the wars David himself should have been fighting.

    C. After Uriah was dead, David took Bathsheba as his wife (2 Sam. 11:6-26).

    D. The lesson for us is that the moment we achieve our dreams is the time we are most vulnerable to an attack.

    E. After a victory, we need to be more dependent on God than we have ever been in our lives.

IX. The Bible says, *"But the thing that David had done displeased the Lord"* (2 Sam. 11:27).

    A. So, the Lord sent the prophet Nathan, who went to David and told him a story about a rich man who stole his poor neighbor's only lamb, killed it, and used it to feed a guest.

B. David said, "Any man who would do such a thing deserves to die!"

C. Nathan said "You are that man" and gave a prophecy that the child conceived by Bathsheba in adultery would die (2 Sam. 12:1-14).

D. I believe that the reason Nathan presented the prophecy in parable form is that God was letting David prescribe his own judgment.

E. If David had been merciful, I believe he would have received mercy in return, but because he showed no mercy to the man in this parable, David passed sentence on himself and received no mercy.

X. After the death of his baby, it says that David comforted Bathsheba, and they conceived another son whom they called Solomon.

A. The Lord sent the prophet Nathan to announce that his name was Jedidiah (2 Sam. 12:25), which means *beloved of the Lord* in Hebrew.

B. God anointed Solomon to be David's replacement as king of Israel (1 Kin. 1:17 and 1 Chr. 28:5).

C. The Bible says there will never be another man who approaches the wisdom and the riches of Solomon.

D. All of this came to a person who was totally outside of God's original plan and purpose.

E. David's relationship with Bathsheba was never God's will, yet He blessed their marriage after they repented.

XI. Maybe you think you have blown it because of bad decisions you have made in the past, but you can't blow it any more than David did.

A. God took the mess David made of his life and worked it together for good—to the extent that he is remembered as a great man.

B. God made an everlasting covenant with David, resulting in blessings to his descendants even when they weren't serving Him.

C. I hope this encourages you.

D. You may have made some less-than-perfect choices, but it is pointless to spend your time regretting the past.

E. It would be wrong to walk away or try to reverse your life and go back.

F. You are where you are because of the choices you have made.

G. The thing to do is humble yourself, seek God, and realize that He can take where you are right now and work everything together for good.

XII. David made some serious mistakes that cost him a great deal of agony—decisions that also cost his family a lot of pain.

   A. He could have beaten himself up over his mistakes, but instead, he trusted God.

   B. He chose to be strong in the grace that is in the Lord (2 Tim. 2:1), which is a great lesson.

   C. I am absolutely convinced that regardless of where you are today or how badly you may have missed God's will for your life, He still has a plan for you.

XIII. The Apostle Paul wrote in his letter to the Romans,

   For the gifts and calling of God are without repentance.
                                                    ROMANS 11:29

   A. God doesn't change, and whatever His purpose for your life was when He created you hasn't changed either.

   B. You might be a long way from where God wants you to be right now, but God can get you where you need to be.

   C. God can take what you have done and figure a way to get you back on track.

   D. You can still get where God planned for you to go.

   E. It doesn't matter what the devil does, and it doesn't matter how much you blow it or mess up—God is able to take whatever you have done to ruin your life and turn it around.

XIV. Your failings are no match for God's grace—they aren't even worthy to mention in the same breath.

   A. You just need to yield to the Lord and say, "God, here I am. Do with me what You want."

   B. God can redeem the last days.

   C. The simple fact that you are reading this study guide shows that God is drawing you and trying to reach out to you.

   D. But you can't do things the way you always have in the past and expect different results.

7. Second Samuel 11:1 says that it was time for kings to go forth to battle, so David should have been out leading his troops. But he stayed home and got away from what God called him to do. When David was running for his life from Saul and it looked like he could die at any moment, he sought God with his whole heart. After he became king, God blessed him and he was more successful than any other king before him, but he stopped seeking after God wholeheartedly. The awesome truth we need to understand here is that success, not failure, is the true test of character. The question is, are we going to seek God as strongly during the good times as we do when we are struggling?

7a.   Why wasn't David seeking God with his whole heart?
Because he wasn't in a situation where he was running for his life and it looked like he could die at any moment

7b.   Success, not failure, is the _____ test of character.
True

7c.   Discussion question: Are you going to seek God as strongly during the good times as you do when you are struggling?
Discussion question

8. When everything is fine, the majority of people tend to forget their need for God—which leads to trouble:

    And it came to pass in an eveningtide, that David arose from off his bed, and walked upon the roof of the king's house: and from the roof he saw a woman washing herself; and the woman was very beautiful to look upon. [3] And David sent and enquired after the woman. And one said, Is not this Bathsheba, the daughter of Eliam, the wife of Uriah the Hittite? [4] And David sent messengers, and took her; and she came in unto him, and he lay with her; for she was purified from her uncleanness: and she returned unto her house. [5] And the woman conceived, and sent and told David, and said, I am with child.

    2 SAMUEL 11:2-5

If David had been doing what God called him to do as king, this temptation would never have come. To cover up their adultery, David plotted the murder of Bathsheba's husband, Uriah—who was one of the mighty men off fighting the wars David himself should have been fighting. After Uriah was dead, David took Bathsheba as his wife (2 Sam. 11:6-26). The lesson for us is that the moment we achieve our dreams is the time we are most vulnerable to an attack. After a victory, we need to be more dependent on God than we have ever been in our lives.

8a. Read 2 Samuel 11:2-5. What do the majority of people tend to do when everything is fine?
     Forget their need for God

8b. True or false: If David had been doing what God called him to do as king, this temptation would never have come.
     True

8c. What did David do to cover up his adultery with Bathsheba?
     He plotted the murder of her husband, Uriah

8d. Then what did he do?
     A. He made public announcement
     B. He honored Uriah for his loyalty and valor
     C. He took Bathsheba as his wife
     D. All of the above
     E. None of the above
     C. He took Bathsheba as his wife

9. The Bible says, *"But the thing that David had done displeased the L*ORD*"* (2 Sam. 11:27). So, the Lord sent the prophet Nathan, who went to David and told him a story about a rich man who stole his poor neighbor's only lamb, killed it, and used it to feed a guest. David said, "Any man who would do such a thing deserves to die!" Nathan said "You are that man" and gave a prophecy that the child conceived by Bathsheba in adultery would die (2 Sam. 12:1-14). I believe that the reason Nathan presented the prophecy in parable form is that God was letting David prescribe his own judgment. If David had been merciful, I believe he would have received mercy in return, but because he showed no mercy to the man in this parable, David passed sentence on himself and received no mercy.

9a.　Discussion question: The fact that Nathan prophesied that David and Bathsheba's child would die, what does that tell you about how God felt about what they did?
　　　Discussion question

9b.　Why does Andrew believe that Nathan presented the prophecy to David in parable form?
　　　Because Andrew believes that God was letting David prescribe his own judgment

9c.　What would have happened if David had been merciful?
　　　A. He would have been better liked
　　　B. He would have been shown mercy
　　　C. He still would have received justice
　　　D. All of the above
　　　E. None of the above
　　　B. He would have been shown mercy

10. After the death of his baby, it says that David comforted Bathsheba, and they conceived another son whom they called Solomon. The Lord sent the prophet Nathan to announce that his name was Jedidiah (2 Sam. 12:25), which means *beloved of the Lord* in Hebrew. God anointed Solomon to be David's replacement as king of Israel (1 Kin. 1:17 and 1 Chr. 28:5). The Bible says there will never be another man who approaches the wisdom and the riches of Solomon. All of this came to a person who was totally outside of God's original plan and purpose. David's relationship with Bathsheba was never God's will, yet He blessed their marriage after they repented.

10a.　How did the Lord feel about Solomon, David and Bathsheba's second son?
　　　A. He tolerated him
　　　B. He felt sorry for him
　　　C. He despised him
　　　D. He envied him
　　　E. He loved him
　　　E. He loved him

10b.　Discussion question: What do you think about how God blessed Solomon, even though He didn't originally approve of David and Bathsheba's relationship?
　　　Discussion question

11. Maybe you think you have blown it because of bad decisions you have made in the past, but you can't blow it any more than David did. God took the mess David made of his life and worked it together for good—to the extent that he is remembered as a great man. God made an everlasting covenant with David, resulting in blessings to his descendants even when they weren't serving Him. I hope this encourages you. You may have made some less-than-perfect choices, but it is pointless to spend your time regretting the past. It would be wrong to walk away or try to reverse your life and go back. You are where you are because of the choices you have made. The thing to do is humble yourself, seek God, and realize that He can take where you are right now and work everything together for good.

11a. How is David remembered?
As a great man

11b. True or false: God's covenant with David resulted in blessings to his descendants even when they weren't serving Him.
True

11c. It would be _____ to walk away or try to reverse your life and go back.
Wrong

11d. What should you do instead?
    A. Humble yourself
    B. Seek God
    C. Realize that He can take where you are right now and work everything together for good
    D. All of the above
    E. None of the above
    D. All of the above

12. David made some serious mistakes that cost him a great deal of agony—decisions that also cost his family a lot of pain. He could have beaten himself up over his mistakes, but instead, he trusted God. He chose to be strong in the grace that is in the Lord (2 Tim. 2:1), which is a great lesson. I am absolutely convinced that regardless of where you are today or how badly you may have missed God's will for your life, He still has a plan for you.

12a. What did David do instead of beat himself up over his mistakes?
He trusted God

12b. According to 2 Timothy 2:1, what should you be strong in?
    A. Numbers
    B. Valor
    C. Odor
    D. Worldly goods and essentials
    E. The grace that is in Christ Jesus
    E. The grace that is in Christ Jesus

12c. Discussion question: Why is it that regardless of how badly you may have missed God's will for your life, He still has a plan for you?
Discussion question

13. The Apostle Paul wrote in his letter to the Romans,

For the gifts and calling of God are without repentance.

ROMANS 11:29

God doesn't change, and whatever His purpose for your life was when He created you hasn't changed either. You might be a long way from where God wants you to be right now, but God can get you where you need to be. God can take what you have done and figure a way to get you back on track. You can still get where God planned for you to go. It doesn't matter what the devil does, and it doesn't matter how much you blow it or mess up—God is able to take whatever you have done to ruin your life and turn it around.

13a. Read Romans 11:29. True or false: Sometimes God changes.
False

13b. You can _____ get where God planned for you to go.
Still

14. Your failings are no match for God's grace—they aren't even worthy to mention in the same breath. You just need to yield to the Lord and say, "God, here I am. Do with me what You want." God can redeem the last days. The simple fact that you are reading this study guide shows that God is drawing you and trying to reach out to you. But you can't do things the way you always have in the past and expect different results.

14a. Discussion question: How do you know this: Your failings are no match for God's grace—they aren't even worthy to mention in the same breath?
Discussion question

14b. The simple fact that you are reading this study guide shows what?
That God is drawing you and trying to reach out to you

14c. You can't do things the way you always have in the past and expect what?
    A. Different results
    B. The same results
    C. Things to be done differently in the future
    D. All of the above
    E. None of the above
    A. Different results

14. Why wasn't David seeking God with his whole heart?

_____

_____

_____

15. Success, not failure, is the _____ test of character.

16. Discussion question: Are you going to seek God as strongly during the good times as you do when you are struggling?

_____

_____

_____

17. Read 2 Samuel 11:2-5. What do the majority of people tend to do when everything is fine?

_____

_____

_____

18. True or false: If David had been doing what God called him to do as king, this temptation would never have come.

19. What did David do to cover up his adultery with Bathsheba?

_____

_____

_____

20. Then what did he do?
    A. He made a public announcement
    B. He honored Uriah for his loyalty and valor
    C. He took Bathsheba as his wife
    D. All of the above
    E. None of the above

21. Discussion question: The fact that Nathan prophesied that David and Bathsheba's child would die, what does that tell you about how God felt about what they did?

_____

_____

_____

22. Why does Andrew believe that Nathan presented the prophecy to David in parable form?

_____

_____

_____

23. What would have happened if David had been merciful?
    A. He would have been better liked
    B. He would have been shown mercy
    C. He still would have received justice
    D. All of the above
    E. None of the above

24. How did the Lord feel about Solomon, David and Bathsheba's second son?
    A. He tolerated him
    B. He felt sorry for him
    C. He despised him
    D. He envied him
    E. He loved him

25. Discussion question: What do you think about how God blessed Solomon, even though He didn't originally approve of David and Bathsheba's relationship?

_____

_____

_____

26. How is David remembered?

_____

_____

_____

27. True or false: God's covenant with David resulted in blessings to his descendants even when they weren't serving Him.

28. It would be _____ to walk away or try to reverse your life and go back.

29. What should you do instead?
    A. Humble yourself
    B. Seek God
    C. Realize that He can take where you are right now and work everything together for good
    D. All of the above
    E. None of the above

30. What did David do instead of beat himself up over his mistakes?

    _____

    _____

    _____

31. According to 2 Timothy 2:1, what should you be strong in?
    A. Numbers
    B. Valor
    C. Odor
    D. Worldly goods and essentials
    E. The grace that is in Christ Jesus

32. Discussion question: Why is it that regardless of how badly you may have missed God's will for your life, He still has a plan for you?

    _____

    _____

    _____

33. Read Romans 11:29. True or false: Sometimes God changes.

34. You can _____ get where God planned for you to go.

35. Discussion question: How do you know this: Your failings are no match for God's grace—they aren't even worthy to mention in the same breath?

_____

_____

_____

36. The simple fact that you are reading this study guide shows what?

_____

_____

_____

37. You can't do things the way you always have in the past and expect what?
   A. Different results
   B. The same results
   C. Things to be done differently in the future
   D. All of the above
   E. None of the above

14. Because he wasn't in a situation where he was running for his life and it looked like he could die at any moment
15. True
16. *Discussion question*
17. Forget their need for God
18. True
19. He plotted the murder of her husband, Uriah
20. C. He took Bathsheba as his wife
21. *Discussion question*
22. Because Andrew believes that God was letting David prescribe his own judgment
23. B. He would have been shown mercy
24. E. He loved him
25. *Discussion question*
26. As a great man
27. True
28. Wrong
29. D. All of the above
30. He trusted God
31. E. The grace that is in Christ Jesus
32. *Discussion question*
33. False
34. Still
35. Discussion question
36. That God is drawing you and trying to reach out to you
37. A. Different results

2 SAMUEL 11:1-27

And it came to pass, after the year was expired, at the time when kings go forth to battle, that David sent Joab, and his servants with him, and all Israel; and they destroyed the children of Ammon, and besieged Rabbah. But David tarried still at Jerusalem. [2] And it came to pass in an eveningtide, that David arose from off his bed, and walked upon the roof of the king's house: and from the roof he saw a woman washing herself; and the woman was very beautiful to look upon. [3] And David sent and enquired after the woman. And one said, Is not this Bathsheba, the daughter of Eliam, the wife of Uriah the Hittite? [4] And David sent messengers, and took her; and she came in unto him, and he lay with her; for she was purified from her uncleanness: and she returned unto her house. [5] And the woman conceived, and sent and told David, and said, I am with child. [6] And David sent to Joab, saying, Send me Uriah the Hittite. And Joab sent Uriah to David. [7] And when Uriah was come unto him, David demanded of him how Joab did, and how the people did, and how the war prospered. [8] And David said to Uriah, Go down to thy house, and wash thy feet. And Uriah departed out of the king's house, and there followed him a mess of meat from the king. [9] But Uriah slept at the door of the king's house with all the servants of his lord, and went not down to his house. [10] And when they had told David, saying, Uriah went not down unto his house, David said unto Uriah, Camest thou not from thy journey? why then didst thou not go down unto thine house? [11] And Uriah said unto David, The ark, and Israel, and Judah, abide in tents; and my lord Joab, and the servants of my lord, are encamped in the open fields; shall I then go into mine house, to eat and to drink, and to lie with my wife? as thou livest, and as thy soul liveth, I will not do this thing. [12] And David said to Uriah, Tarry here to day also, and to morrow I will let thee depart. So Uriah abode in Jerusalem that day, and the morrow. [13] And when David had called him, he did eat and drink before him; and he made him drunk: and at even he went out to lie on his bed with the servants of his lord, but went not down to his house. [14] And it came to pass in the morning, that David wrote a letter to Joab, and sent it by the hand of Uriah. [15] And he wrote in the letter, saying, Set ye Uriah in the forefront of the hottest battle, and retire ye from him, that he may be smitten, and die. [16] And it came to pass, when Joab observed the city, that he assigned Uriah unto a place where he knew that valiant men were. [17] And the men of the city went out, and fought with Joab: and there fell some of the people of the servants of David; and Uriah the Hittite died also. [18] Then Joab sent and told David all the things concerning the war; [19] And charged the messenger, saying, When thou hast made an end of telling the matters of the war unto the king, [20] And if so be that the king's wrath arise, and he say unto thee, Wherefore approached ye so nigh unto the city when ye did fight? knew ye not that they would shoot from the wall? [21] Who smote Abimelech the son of Jerubbesheth? did not a woman cast a piece of a millstone upon him from the wall, that he died in Thebez? why went ye nigh the wall? then say thou, Thy servant Uriah the Hittite is dead also. [22] So the messenger went, and came and shewed David all that Joab had sent him for. [23] And the messenger said unto David, Surely the men prevailed against us, and came out unto us into the field, and we were upon them even unto the entering of the gate. [24] And the shooters shot from off the wall upon thy servants; and some of the king's servants be dead, and thy servant Uriah the Hittite is dead also. [25] Then David said unto the messenger, Thus shalt thou say unto Joab, Let not this thing displease thee, for the sword devoureth one as well as another: make thy battle more strong against the city, and overthrow it: and encourage thou him. [26] And when the wife of Uriah heard that Uriah her husband was dead, she mourned for her husband. [27] And when the mourning was past, David sent and fetched her to his house, and she became his wife, and bare him a son. But the thing that David had done displeased the LORD.

2 SAMUEL 12:1-14
And the Lord sent Nathan unto David. And he came unto him, and said unto him, There were two men in one city; the one rich, and the other poor. [2] The rich man had exceeding many flocks and herds: [3] But the poor man had nothing, save one little ewe lamb, which he had bought and nourished up: and it grew up together with him, and with his children; it did eat of his own meat, and drank of his own cup, and lay in his bosom, and was unto him as a daughter. [4] And there came a traveller unto the rich man, and he spared to take of his own flock and of his own herd, to dress for the wayfaring man that was come unto him; but took the poor man's lamb, and dressed it for the man that was come to him. [5] And David's anger was greatly kindled against the man; and he said to Nathan, As the LORD liveth, the man that hath done this thing shall surely die: [6] And he shall restore the lamb fourfold, because he did this thing, and because he had no pity. [7] And Nathan said to David, Thou art the man. Thus saith the LORD God of Israel, I anointed thee king over Israel, and I delivered thee out of the hand of Saul; [8] And I gave thee thy master's house, and thy master's wives into thy bosom, and gave thee the house of Israel and of Judah; and if that had been too little, I would moreover have given unto thee such and such things. [9] Wherefore hast thou despised the commandment of the LORD, to do evil in his sight? thou hast killed Uriah the Hittite with the sword, and hast taken his wife to be thy wife, and hast slain him with the sword of the children of Ammon. [10] Now therefore the sword shall never depart from thine house; because thou hast despised me, and hast taken the wife of Uriah the Hittite to be thy wife. [11] Thus saith the LORD, Behold, I will raise up evil against thee out of thine own house, and I will take thy wives before thine eyes, and give them unto thy neighbour, and he shall lie with thy wives in the sight of this sun. [12] For thou didst it secretly: but I will do this thing before all Israel, and before the sun. [13] And David said unto Nathan, I have sinned against the LORD. And Nathan said unto David, The LORD also hath put away thy sin; thou shalt not die. [14] Howbeit, because by this deed thou hast given great occasion to the enemies of the LORD to blaspheme, the child also that is born unto thee shall surely die.

JAMES 2:13

For he shall have judgment without mercy, that hath shewed no mercy; and mercy rejoiceth against judgment.

2 SAMUEL 22:26

With the merciful thou wilt shew thyself merciful, and with the upright man thou wilt shew thyself upright.

2 SAMUEL 12:25

And he sent by the hand of Nathan the prophet; and he called his name Jedidiah, because of the LORD.

1 KINGS 1:17

And she said unto him, My lord, thou swarest by the LORD thy God unto thine handmaid, saying, Assuredly Solomon thy son shall reign after me, and he shall sit upon my throne.

1 CHRONICLES 28:5

And of all my sons, (for the LORD hath given me many sons,) he hath chosen Solomon my son to sit upon the throne of the kingdom of the LORD over Israel.

1 KINGS 10:21

And all king Solomon's drinking vessels were of gold, and all the vessels of the house of the forest of Lebanon were of pure gold; none were of silver: it was nothing accounted of in the days of Solomon.

2 CHRONICLES 1:12

Wisdom and knowledge is granted unto thee; and I will give thee riches, and wealth, and honour, such as none of the kings have had that have been before thee, neither shall there any after thee have the like.

2 SAMUEL 13:10-14

And Amnon said unto Tamar, Bring the meat into the chamber, that I may eat of thine hand. And Tamar took the cakes which she had made, and brought them into the chamber to Amnon her brother. [11] And when she had brought them unto him to eat, he took hold of her, and said unto her, Come lie with me, my sister. [12] And she answered him, Nay, my brother, do not force me; for no such thing ought to be done in Israel: do not thou this folly. [13] And I, whither shall I cause my shame to go? and as for thee, thou shalt be as one of the fools in Israel. Now therefore, I pray thee, speak unto the king; for he will not withhold me from thee. [14] Howbeit he would not hearken unto her voice: but, being stronger than she, forced her, and lay with her.

2 SAMUEL 13:28-29
Now Absalom had commanded his servants, saying, Mark ye now when Amnon's heart is merry with wine, and when I say unto you, Smite Amnon; then kill him, fear not: have not I commanded you? be courageous, and be valiant. [29] And the servants of Absalom did unto Amnon as Absalom had commanded. Then all the king's sons arose, and every man gat him up upon his mule, and fled.

2 SAMUEL 15:10
But Absalom sent spies throughout all the tribes of Israel, saying, As soon as ye hear the sound of the trumpet, then ye shall say, Absalom reigneth in Hebron.

2 TIMOTHY 2:1
Thou therefore, my son, be strong in the grace that is in Christ Jesus.

ROMANS 11:29
For the gifts and calling of God are without repentance.

A LIVING SACRIFICE

LESSON 3.1

I beseech you therefore, brethren, by the mercies of God, that ye present your bodies a living sacrifice, holy, acceptable unto God, which is your reasonable service.

ROMANS 12:1

God used this passage of Scripture to change my life. This is the very first verse that God ever spoke into my heart and made come alive. For almost eighteen months leading up to that revelation, I had been seeking God and studying the Bible to find His will. I was preparing the ground. This brings up an important point I can't overemphasize: God won't reveal His will for your life until you are ready to receive it.

God doesn't show us the full scope of His plan all at once. He doesn't show us the end from the beginning. He will start pointing us in a direction and moving us toward it, but He won't show us everything all at once, because we aren't ready to embrace what He has to say. Seeing the full scope of God's will all at once would overwhelm us. We might think we are incapable of doing what He has planned for us, or we might become so impatient that we would never stay the course long enough for God to prepare us to carry out our calling. It isn't that God is hesitant to show us His will—sometimes it just takes Him a while to bring us to a place where we are ready to receive it.

My preparation was seeking the Lord and being *consumed* with finding His will for my life. This hunger to know God's will led me to the verses in Romans 12—the revelation of what those verses meant led to an encounter with God on March 23, 1968. That encounter totally changed my life. And it all started with simply wanting to find God's will.

The first stage of finding God's particular will for your life is to become a living sacrifice, holy and acceptable unto Him (Rom. 12:1). From an eternal perspective, what you do for an occupation is incidental. The Lord doesn't want your *service* as much as He wants *you*. He loves you more than He loves what you can do for Him. Now, that's an important point to make, because in our day and age—especially in the type of church atmosphere that I grew up in—it's all about service: a push to *do* something for God. It's true that you were created for God's pleasure and glory, but *God's acceptance of you is not related to what you do for Him.* The Lord sacrificed Himself so He could have *you*, not your *service.*

When I was seeking God in 1968, I wasn't even thinking about being a preacher. I was asking God if He wanted me to be a teacher, doctor, or something like that. One of the things the Lord spoke to me was that I was missing it by seeking Him for a vocation. He told me, "I want you. If I get you, then I'll be able to use you however I want to." I was praying "O God, use me. Show me what You want me to do. God, should I do this or that?" The Lord finally spoke to me and said, "The reason I haven't used you is because you aren't *usable.* Quit praying that I'll use you; pray 'God, make me usable.'"

Besides, God wants to use you more than you want to be used. If you make yourself a living sacrifice and commit your life to the Lord, I guarantee you, He will start developing your talents and directing you. As soon as you get usable, God will use you. Jesus said,

> *The harvest truly is plenteous, but the labourers are few; [38] Pray ye therefore the Lord of the harvest, that he will send forth labourers into his harvest.*
> MATTHEW 9:37-38

God is looking for people He can use, but the problem is most people aren't usable. Of course, making yourself usable doesn't mean that you try to go out and accomplish God's plan in your own strength and ability. Look how Jesus approached His ministry:

> *Now when he was in Jerusalem at the passover, in the feast day, many believed in his name, when they saw the miracles which he did. [24] But Jesus did not commit himself unto them, because he knew all men, [25] And needed not that any should testify of man: for he knew what was in man.*
> JOHN 2:23-25

What would we do if this happened today? Let's say, for instance, a preacher came to town and suddenly people were being raised from the dead, and miracles were happening by the hundreds. What would the average preacher do in that situation? He would probably mobilize the people, put literature in their hands, and send them out to witness to others about the power of God they were seeing. Then he would call the television stations, advertise, and try to take advantage of what was happening.

This passage describes a multitude of people who were willing to acknowledge that Jesus was the Christ. Yet Jesus did not commit Himself to them. He didn't partner with them because He knew what was in man. Jesus didn't want those people talking about Him because He knew they weren't ready. For one thing, they weren't born again. They weren't filled with the Holy Spirit either. Even after His disciples had spent three-and-a-half years with Him and had seen Him rise from the dead, the last thing Jesus told them was, "Don't go tell anybody I'm resurrected from the dead until you receive the power of the Holy Spirit. Then you'll be empowered to be My witnesses."

Jesus is more concerned about the *quality* of ministry than He is the *quantity* of ministry. We're almost completely the opposite. Today when someone is born again, we pat them on the back and immediately send them out to tell everybody. That isn't the way God wants the church to operate.

You need to be prepared. You need to get to where you aren't ministering out of your own ability—but through the power of God. It takes a while for that to happen. Jesus wouldn't commit Himself to those people, because He didn't want anyone to speak out of their own ability. The majority of people today who represent God are just teaching things they have heard someone else say. Their hearts may be good and they may mean well, but their teaching is just the teaching of man. It's not the power of the Holy Spirit; therefore, it causes problems.

This goes right along with the idea that God wants you before He wants your service. If God doesn't have your heart, then why would He want to reveal His purpose to you? You would just go out in your own human ability and make a mess of things, trying to fulfill His will. He loves you too much for that. Sure, the Lord is concerned about the witness you present to others, but it is also out of love and concern for you that He doesn't want you stepping out solely in your own power.

Fight in God's Strength

Some wonderful things go along with finding God's will. Earlier, I mentioned a sense of satisfaction, peace, and joy that you will never experience unless you find God's will. When you find God's plan and walk in the center of His will, it's like pinning a huge target on yourself. Satan fights against those who try to advance the kingdom of God. You are going to be met with opposition while fulfilling God's purpose for your life. You will face challenges. If God doesn't have your heart so He can mold it to meet your needs and give you faith to overcome obstacles, you're going to be in trouble. The wiles of the Enemy and the darts that come against you would destroy you if you found God's will and moved out in your own strength to accomplish it.

The reason that some people haven't bumped into the devil is because they're going in the same direction! They haven't had any great problems in life because they aren't a threat. The good news is that as far as we can tell in Scripture, demons don't reproduce. So, either there was a bunch of demons per person back in Adam and Eve's day or there's a shortage of demons today. Personally, I believe there's a shortage of demons. I believe that Satan is short-handed, and I don't believe—as some claim—that every person has their own personal demon.

Satan taught a lot of us a couple wrong things a long time ago, so now we're doing a wonderful job messing up our own lives. He can leave us alone because we're doing a bang-up job on our own. Some people have probably inspired the devil. I bet the devil sometimes sits down and takes notes and says, "Oh, I never thought of that one." Seriously, though, when you find God's will and the anointing of God flows through you and people's lives are impacted, I can guarantee that you are going to face some form of demonic activity.

Satan puts a priority on people who are in the center of God's will, making an impact, and causing his earthly kingdom damage. It's just like being in a battle: An army that is attacked on one flank will shift forces to reinforce that area and repel the attack. In the same way, when you start fulfilling God's will for your life, there is going to be opposition. Satan will marshal his forces against you to protect himself. God loves you too much to reveal His will to you and put you on the front lines when you are not prepared to meet the challenge.

I hope you are getting this: *One of the main reasons God doesn't automatically reveal His will to everyone is that He loves them too much to put them at risk.* He doesn't want you out there trying to advance His kingdom in your flesh, unable to deal with the opposition and criticism that would come against you. He doesn't want you to be destroyed. He's not willing to sacrifice you. God doesn't see you as a disposable commodity. He doesn't use people like you would a soda cup: suck on the straw until you hear *sluuurrrp*, then throw the cup away, and go get another one. God loves you too much to use you like that. He loves you more than He loves what you can do for Him.

OUTLINE • 3.1

I. The very first verse that God ever spoke into my heart and made come alive was Romans 12:1:

> *I beseech you therefore, brethren, by the mercies of God, that ye present your bodies a living sacrifice, holy, acceptable unto God, which is your reasonable service.*

A. For almost eighteen months leading up to that revelation, I had been seeking God and studying the Bible to find His will.

B. This brings up an important point I can't overemphasize: God won't reveal His will for your life until you are ready to receive it.

C. He will start pointing you in a direction and moving you toward it, but He won't show you everything all at once, because you aren't ready to embrace what He has to say—it would overwhelm you.

   i. You might think you are incapable of doing what He has planned for you, or you might become so impatient that you would never stay the course long enough for God to prepare you to carry out your calling.

D. It isn't that God is hesitant to show you His will—sometimes it just takes Him a while to bring you to a place where you are ready to receive it.

E. My hunger to know God's will led me to the verses in Romans 12—the revelation of what those verses meant led to an encounter with God on March 23, 1968.

II. The first stage of finding God's particular will for your life is to become a living sacrifice, holy and acceptable unto Him (Rom. 12:1).

A. He loves you more than He loves what you can do for Him.

B. It's true that you were created for God's pleasure and glory, but *His acceptance of you is not related to what you do for Him.*

C. The Lord sacrificed Himself so He could have *you*, not your *service*.

D. One of the things the Lord told me was, "I want you. If I get you, then I'll be able to use you however I want to."

E. I was praying "O God, use me. Show me what You want me to do. God, should I do this or that?" and the Lord finally spoke to me and said, "The reason I haven't used you is because you aren't *usable*. Quit praying that I'll use you; pray 'God, make me usable.'"

F. God wants to use you more than you want to be used.

G. If you make yourself a living sacrifice and commit your life to the Lord, I guarantee you, He will start developing your talents and directing you—as soon as you get usable, God will use you.

III.   The problem is most people aren't usable.

    A. Making yourself usable doesn't mean that you try to go out and accomplish God's plan in your own strength and ability.

Now when he was in Jerusalem at the passover, in the feast day, many believed in his name, when they saw the miracles which he did. [24] But Jesus did not commit himself unto them, because he knew all men, [25] And needed not that any should testify of man: for he knew what was in man.

JOHN 2:23-25

    B. This passage describes a multitude of people who were willing to acknowledge that Jesus was the Christ, yet Jesus did not commit Himself to them, because He knew they weren't ready.

        i.   They weren't born again.

        ii. They weren't filled with the Holy Spirit either.

        iii Even after His disciples had spent three-and-a-half years with Him and had seen Him rise from the dead, the last thing Jesus told them was, "Don't go tell anybody I'm resurrected from the dead until you receive the power of the Holy Spirit. Then you'll be empowered to be My witnesses."

    C. Jesus is more concerned about the *quality* of ministry than He is the *quantity* of ministry.

IV.   You need to get to where you aren't ministering out of your own ability—but through the power of God, and it takes a while for that to happen.

    A. The majority of people today who represent God are just teaching things they have heard someone else say.

    B. Their hearts may be good and they may mean well, but their teaching is not by the power of the Holy Spirit; therefore, it causes problems.

    C. Sure, the Lord is concerned about the witness you present to others, but it is also out of love and concern for you that He doesn't want you stepping out solely in your own power.

V.   Satan fights against those who try to advance the kingdom of God.

    A. You are going to be met with opposition while fulfilling God's purpose for your life.

    B. The reason that some people haven't bumped into the devil is because they're going in the same direction—they haven't had any great problems in life because they aren't a threat.

    C. Personally, I believe that Satan is short-handed.

D. Satan taught a lot of people a couple wrong things a long time ago, so now they're doing a wonderful job messing up their own lives.

E. Satan puts a priority on people who are in the center of God's will, making an impact, and causing his earthly kingdom damage.

  i. It's just like being in a battle: An army that is attacked on one flank will shift forces to reinforce that area and repel the attack.

F. One of the main reasons God doesn't automatically reveal His will to you is that He doesn't want you out there trying to advance His kingdom in your flesh, unable to deal with the opposition and criticism that would come against you.

G. He's not willing to sacrifice you—He doesn't see you as a disposable commodity.

1. The very first verse that God ever spoke into my heart and made come alive was Romans 12:1:

> *I beseech you therefore, brethren, by the mercies of God, that ye present your bodies*
> *a living sacrifice, holy, acceptable unto God, which is your reasonable service.*

For almost eighteen months leading up to that revelation, I had been seeking God and studying the Bible to find His will. This brings up an important point I can't overemphasize: God won't reveal His will for your life until you are ready to receive it. He will start pointing you in a direction and moving you toward it, but He won't show you everything all at once, because you aren't ready to embrace what He has to say—it would overwhelm you. You might think you are incapable of doing what He has planned for you, or you might become so impatient that you would never stay the course long enough for God to prepare you to carry out your calling. It isn't that God is hesitant to show you His will—sometimes it just takes Him a while to bring you to a place where you are ready to receive it. My hunger to know God's will led me to the verses in Romans 12—the revelation of what those verses meant led to an encounter with God on March 23, 1968.

1a.   What can't Andrew overemphasize?
      That God won't reveal His will for your life until you are ready to receive it

1b.   Discussion question: What's wrong with thinking you're incapable of doing what God has planned for you?
      Discussion question

1c.   True or false: God is hesitant to show you His will.
      False

2. The first stage of finding God's particular will for your life is to become a living sacrifice, holy and acceptable unto Him (Rom. 12:1). He loves you more than He loves what you can do for Him. It's true that you were created for God's pleasure and glory, but *His acceptance of you is not related to what you do for Him.* The Lord sacrificed Himself so He could have *you*, not your *service.* One of the things the Lord told me was, "I want you. If I get you, then I'll be able to use you however I want to." I was praying "O God, use me. Show me what You want me to do. God, should I do this or that?" and the Lord finally spoke to me and said, "The reason I haven't used you is because you aren't *usable.* Quit praying that I'll use you; pray 'God, make me usable.'" God wants to use you more than you want to be used. If you make yourself a living sacrifice and commit your life to the Lord, I guarantee you, He will start developing your talents and directing you—as soon as you get usable, God will use you.

2a.   Read Romans 12:1. What is the first step to finding God's will for your life?
A. Giving up popcorn and sodas
B. Making sure there is no sin in your life
C. Becoming a living sacrifice, holy and acceptable unto Him
D. All of the above
E. None of the above
C. Becoming a living sacrifice, holy and acceptable unto Him

2b.   God loves you more than what?
What you do for Him

2c.   What did God do so He could have you?
He sacrificed Himself

2d.   What should you pray instead of "God, use me"?
A. God, I am useless
B. God, only use me under certain conditions
C. God, don't use me
D. God, make me usable
E. God, use that person instead of me
D. God, make me usable

2e.   True or false: God wants to use you just as much as you want to be used.
False

2f.   What will God do if you make yourself a living sacrifice and commit your life to the Lord?
He will start developing your talents and directing you—as soon as you get usable, God will use you

3. The problem is most people aren't usable. Making yourself usable doesn't mean that you try to go out and accomplish God's plan in your own strength and ability.

> *Now when he was in Jerusalem at the passover, in the feast day, many believed in his name, when they saw the miracles which he did. [24] But Jesus did not commit himself unto them, because he knew all men, [25] And needed not that any should testify of man: for he knew what was in man.*
>
> JOHN 2:23-25

This passage describes a multitude of people who were willing to acknowledge that Jesus was the Christ, yet Jesus did not commit Himself to them, because He knew they weren't ready. They weren't born again. They weren't filled with the Holy Spirit either. Even after His disciples had spent three-and-a-half years with Him and had seen Him rise from the dead, the last thing Jesus told them was, "Don't go tell anybody I'm resurrected from the dead until you receive the power of the Holy Spirit. Then you'll be empowered to be My witnesses." Jesus is more concerned about the *quality* of ministry than He is the *quantity* of ministry.

3a.   What's one way to not make yourself usable?
      Trying to go out and accomplish God's plan in your own strength and ability

3b.   Discussion question: Read John 2:23-25. Why do you think the fact that these people believed in Jesus' name didn't change Jesus' decision not to commit to them?
      Discussion question

3c.   True or false: Jesus is more concerned about the quality of ministry than He is the quantity of ministry.
      True

4. You need to get to where you aren't ministering out of your own ability—but through the power of God, and it takes a while for that to happen. The majority of people today who represent God are just teaching things they have heard someone else say. Their hearts may be good and they may mean well, but their teaching is not by the power of the Holy Spirit; therefore, it causes problems. Sure, the Lord is concerned about the witness you present to others, but it is also out of love and concern for you that He doesn't want you stepping out solely in your own power.

4a. What takes a while to happen?
A. Ministering with the support of people
B. Ministering with enough financial backing
C. Ministering through the power of God
D. All of the above
E. None of the above
C. Ministering through the power of God

4b. What is the reason God doesn't want you stepping out solely in your own power?
A. Because He wants to share the glory with you
B. It's out of His love and concern for you
C. Because He wants to micromanage you
D. The answer varies per person
E. There really isn't a good enough reason
B. It's out of His love and concern for you

5. Satan fights against those who try to advance the kingdom of God. You are going to be met with opposition while fulfilling God's purpose for your life. The reason that some people haven't bumped into the devil is because they're going in the same direction—they haven't had any great problems in life because they aren't a threat. Personally, I believe that Satan is short-handed. Satan taught a lot of people a couple wrong things a long time ago, so now they're doing a wonderful job messing up their own lives. Satan puts a priority on people who are in the center of God's will, making an impact, and causing his earthly kingdom damage. It's just like being in a battle: An army that is attacked on one flank will shift forces to reinforce that area and repel the attack. One of the main reasons God doesn't automatically reveal His will to you is that He doesn't want you out there trying to advance His kingdom in your flesh, unable to deal with the opposition and criticism that would come against you. He's not willing to sacrifice you—He doesn't see you as a disposable commodity.

5a.   You're going to be met with what while fulfilling God's purpose for your life?
Opposition

5b.   Discussion question: Why is it important to know that Satan is short-handed?
Discussion question

5c.   True or false: Satan is messing up everyone's lives.
False

5d.   What's one of the main reasons God doesn't automatically reveal His will to you?
He doesn't want you out there trying to advance His kingdom in your flesh, unable to deal with the opposition and criticism that would come against you

5e.   What isn't God willing to sacrifice?
A.   Money
B.   Time
C.   Effort
D.   You
E.   Animals
D.   You

DISCIPLESHIP QUESTIONS • 3.1

1. What can't Andrew overemphasize?

   _____

   _____

   _____

2. Discussion question: What's wrong with thinking you're incapable of doing what God has planned for you?

   _____

   _____

   _____

3. True or false: God is hesitant to show you His will.

4. Read Romans 12:1. What is the first step to finding God's will for your life?
   A. Giving up popcorn and sodas
   B. Making sure there is no sin in your life
   C. Becoming a living sacrifice, holy and acceptable unto Him
   D. All of the above
   E. None of the above

5. God loves you more than what?

   _____

   _____

   _____

6. What did God do so He could have you?

   _____

   _____

   _____

7. What should you pray instead of "God, use me"?
    A. God, I am useless
    B. God, only use me under certain conditions
    C. God, don't use me
    D. God, make me usable
    E. God, use that person instead of me

8. True or false: God wants to use you just as much as you want to be used.

9. What will God do if you make yourself a living sacrifice and commit your life to the Lord?

_____

_____

_____

10. What's one way to not make yourself usable?

_____

_____

_____

11. Discussion question: Read John 2:23-25. Why do you think the fact that these people believed in Jesus' name didn't change Jesus' decision not to commit to them?

_____

_____

_____

12. True or false: Jesus is more concerned about the quality of ministry than He is the quantity of ministry.

13. What takes a while to happen?
    A. Ministering with the support of people
    B. Ministering with enough financial backing
    C. Ministering through the power of God
    D. All of the above
    E. None of the above

14. What is the reason God doesn't want you stepping out solely in your own power?
    A. Because He wants to share the glory with you
    B. It's out of His love and concern for you
    C. Because He wants to micromanage you
    D. The answer varies per person
    E. There really isn't a good enough reason

15. You're going to be met with what while fulfilling God's purpose for your life?

    _____

    _____

    _____

16. Discussion question: Why is it important to know that Satan is short-handed?

    _____

    _____

    _____

17. True or false: Satan is messing up everyone's lives.

18. What's one of the main reasons God doesn't automatically reveal His will to you?

    _____

    _____

    _____

19. What isn't God willing to sacrifice?
    A. Money
    B. Time
    C. Effort
    D. You
    E. Animals

ANSWER KEY • 3.1

1. That God won't reveal His will for your life until you are ready to receive it
2. *Discussion question*
3. False
4. C. Becoming a living sacrifice, holy and acceptable unto Him
5. What you do for Him
6. He sacrificed Himself
7. D. God, make me usable
8. False
9. He will start developing your talents and directing you—as soon as you get usable, God will use you
10. Trying to go out and accomplish God's plan in your own strength and ability
11. *Discussion question*
12. True
13. C. Ministering through the power of God
14. B. It's out of His love and concern for you
15. Opposition
16. *Discussion question*
17. False
18. He doesn't want you out there trying to advance His kingdom in your flesh, unable to deal with the opposition and criticism that would come against you
19. D. You

ROMANS 12:1

I beseech you therefore, brethren, by the mercies of God, that ye present your bodies a living sacrifice, holy, acceptable unto God, which is your reasonable service.

MATTHEW 9:37-38

Then saith he unto his disciples, The harvest truly is plenteous, but the labourers are few; [38] Pray ye therefore the Lord of the harvest, that he will send forth labourers into his harvest.

JOHN 2:23-25

Now when he was in Jerusalem at the passover, in the feast day, many believed in his name, when they saw the miracles which he did. [24] But Jesus did not commit himself unto them, because he knew all men, [25] And needed not that any should testify of man: for he knew what was in man.

LESSON 3.2

To become a living sacrifice, you have to die to yourself and your own selfish ambitions. A sacrifice is something you place on the altar. It doesn't give instructions; it is at the mercy of the person doing the sacrificing. The sacrificer can do anything he wants with it. Dying to one's *self* isn't normal. It isn't what fallen human beings naturally desire.

In case you haven't noticed, sweet little babies don't give a rip about anything but their own needs. They scream and cry to wake mom up in the middle of the night to be fed—oblivious to the fact that mommy just went through labor and is exhausted. Babies will do whatever it takes to get what they want, when they want it, and they don't care one bit how it affects others. Babies think they are the center of the universe. Every one of us came into the world exactly that way, and sad to say, a majority of us are *still* that way.

We might not fall on the floor and suck our thumb or throw a fit, but we still act in selfish ways. Adults have different ways of being self-centered—like turning a shoulder to their spouse that is cold enough to form icicles. The natural tendency of fallen human beings is to think that the world revolves around them. This selfish tendency is Satan's beachhead into your life. It's how he gains access to you.

Satan's temptation against Adam and Eve was to get them to think about themselves. Basically, his temptation was saying to them, "God isn't thinking about you; He's keeping something from you. You could be more like God." In truth, however, God had created a perfect world for Adam and Eve, and there wasn't a single reason for them to be upset. The Garden of Eden was perfect. God Almighty walked with Adam and Eve in the cool of the evening. He gave them honor and respect. Everything was *absolutely* perfect, but Satan made them think that God was holding something back. Adam and Eve rejected God because they didn't think that what they had was good enough—they wanted more.

All human beings start out selfish, but we don't have to stay that way. Prior to my encounter with the Lord in 1968, I was doing all the *right* things for all the *wrong* reasons. I was an absolute hypocrite and didn't even realize it. As far as I knew, I was the most religious kid in our church. I led two or three people a week to the Lord, I started a special youth visitation, I went to the adult visitation, I witnessed to people—I did everything I could. I lived at church and I was seeking God with everything I knew, but the Lord showed me that I was doing it all for myself and a little pat on the back.

On March 23, 1968, God pulled back a curtain and showed me that my heart was all wrong. He showed me that I was selfish and had not been seeking Him with pure motives. We had a prayer meeting every Saturday night. And here I was, *an eighteen-year-old boy meeting every Saturday night to pray with my friends*—that should give you an indication of how religious I was! We were in this prayer meeting joking around, when the youth director of our church came in and dropped to his knees on the floor of the pastor's study. He started praying and crying out to God for about forty-five minutes. During his prayer, I was kneeling down across the room, but instead of enjoying his prayer or communing with God, I was caught up in myself. *How rude*, I thought, *He just came in here, and now he's praying on and on. What am I going to pray?* I told myself, "There won't be anything left to say by the time he finishes! Everybody is going to think I'm carnal and don't love God."

I was thinking these things, when I suddenly realized what an absolute hypocrite I was. I saw how self-centered my whole life had been. I don't know how it happened; it was supernatural, but it was like God just pulled a curtain back. I saw how everything I thought I had been doing for the Lord was actually for my own benefit. I started confessing all of the self-centered things I was seeing about myself. I turned myself inside out in front of my best friends and all the leaders of the church. I thought nobody was ever going to want to be around me again after hearing the things I was revealing—all of the lust and hate that was in my heart, and the way I thought of other people. I ruined my reputation, but I didn't care. I knew I needed to get right with God.

Before this experience, I had been proud of my performance. Now I saw my self-righteousness from God's perspective and thought He was about to kill me. I was just trying to confess everything I could think of, so when He killed me, I could go to heaven. I thought God was seeing all of that junk for the first time—just like I was. I prayed and confessed for about an hour and a half. It was probably the first time in my life I had prayed more than fifteen minutes at a time.

When I was through, there was nothing left to say, nothing more I could give, nothing left to confess. I made myself a living sacrifice that night. I humbled myself. I saw that God was righteous and I was unrighteous. I expected God to kill me because of how unrighteous I was. But instead of wrath and rejection, the tangible love of God came over me and changed my life. It was so real! I'm not sure what happened during the next four-and-a-half months, but I never slept more than an hour at a time, and I never sat down to eat a meal; I just ate enough to keep me going. I was excited—I couldn't sleep knowing how much God loved me! How could I sit down and eat when I could be reading the Bible?

Experiencing God's love transformed my life. Instead of the rejection and punishment I thought was coming, God showed me that He loved me—and I knew it had nothing to do with me. For the first time in my life, I saw that I was a "zero with the rim knocked off." I found God's love and realized it was solely according to His grace. It had nothing to do with my goodness or badness. God just loved me. Learning this truth totally changed me.

Not everybody is going to have the same kind of dramatic encounter that I did, but everybody needs to have a similar experience—a time when you make the decision to quit sitting on the throne of your life, trying to determine your own future. We become a sacrifice when we hand over control, which is primarily what God wants to accomplish in all of us. Until we reach that place, God can't reveal His perfect will—or He certainly can't reveal the entirety of it—because we would go out and try to do it in our own strength and would end up getting hurt or hurting others.

God wants your heart more than He wants your service. You need to run up a white flag of surrender and say, "God, I'm yours. I'll do *anything* you want." I guarantee you that God's plan for you is better than your plan for yourself. It will take a period of time for you to be able to learn God's plan and for Him to work some things out in you. The Lord will start you on the most adventurous path you could ever dream. Life will be better than you could ever plan for yourself.

Yielding to the Lord isn't a one-time decision. The initial resolution begins the process, but God can't deal with all of your flesh in one moment. You have to keep making the choice to surrender. The only way for you to never have another problem with your flesh is for you to *physically die*. As long as you are breathing, you have a self, and that carnal nature is going to seek to reassert its desires.

I haven't been perfect since March 23, 1968, when I surrendered my life to God. I haven't always loved God flawlessly and avoided all selfishness. But I made a commitment with all of my heart that night. As soon as I see selfishness rise up in my life, I repent. I've had to say, "Whoops, there's *self* coming back up again. Father, I'm not going that way. Thank You for showing me." I've had to get back on track, but I've never lost my commitment. I committed myself to God in 1968 and have not been uncommitted since. I haven't always lived up to my commitment, but I've never had to start over again.

Today most people just commit a little bit. Then they do something in absolute rebellion against God and have to come back and recommit. Their lives are up and down like a yo-yo. But we can reach a place where we literally turn everything over to God, and that's all there is to it—a place where no matter what God tells us to do, we will do it without discussion.

When the Lord first called Jamie and me to go to Pritchett, Colorado, I didn't have any desire to go there. It was a puny town of 144 people, thirty miles away from the next largest town of 1,000. As a matter of fact, the first time we drove through Pritchett, we were with some friends of ours, and I started laughing and saying, "Don, I think God's calling you here." I said, "Thus saith the Lord…" and I started joking with him about being called to Pritchett. But it wasn't two months later that *I* was living there!

I had some resistance to the idea, but the moment I was sure God wanted me to do it, I did it. I didn't understand everything. And going to pastor a church of 10 people in a town of 144 wasn't a steppingstone to anything. The only way you leave a situation like that is feet first. But I knew God wanted me to do it, so I did. Once I committed to following God's leading to go to Pritchett, God put His desires in my heart, and I fell in love with the place. I loved Pritchett and had a great time there.

A few times in my life, I have struggled to know if what I was feeling led to do was really God. But once I knew it was God's will, it was nonnegotiable for me—I just did it. I have discovered that most people aren't like that. It's one of the reasons God hasn't revealed His will to them yet. It's also the reason they are struggling. It solves a lot of problems when you figure out there's only one God—and you aren't Him! As long as you are playing God in your life, picking and choosing what you do, you aren't a living sacrifice.

The heart of God's will for you is to be a living sacrifice, committed unto Him. Once you reach that place, you will have to rebel against God to keep from seeing His good, acceptable, and perfect will come to pass in your life (Rom. 12:2). God doesn't need a silver vessel; He's looking for a surrendered one. Commit your life to Him, and He will promote you in whatever area He wants you to go. You will prosper and have the favor of God. Things will work better than they ever did when you were the one calling the shots. Believe it or not, God is smarter than you! God knows more than you do. He can direct your life better than you can (Jer. 10:23), so don't lean unto your own understanding (Prov. 3:5).

Fully submitting to God is the starting place. You can't get around this step. Most people want to skip this rung and move on up to the top of the ladder—they want to stride right into the center of God's will and see great things happen. You're not going to get far that way. The reason we have people in ministry who wind up committing adultery and stealing money is because they didn't take the time to build a foundation of character and integrity. They didn't wait on God to promote them, so fame corrupted them. Don't make that mistake by trying to get around becoming a living sacrifice. Selfishness is Satan's inroad to your life; it's how he gains access to you.

Most people don't trust God to advance them in life because they're too busy trying to advance themselves. In general, we demand respect and assert our rights in an attempt to make everyone around us realize how important we are. This is pretty much the opposite of being a living sacrifice. Being committed to God doesn't mean we lay down like a doormat every time we are confronted with a problem. If God tells us to do something to change our circumstances, we need to do it. I'm just saying that we shouldn't be motivated by selfish desires.

Being a living sacrifice is the first step in finding God's will. It would really jump-start your spiritual life to get off the throne and say, "Jesus, I want *You* to control my life." Still, it's a process. If you are living a totally selfish life right now, you have a lot of momentum built up in that direction. You can't make a complete U-turn instantly. If the Lord suddenly turned you around, it would be a disaster—like trying to flip a U-turn while going sixty-five miles per hour on the highway. It's going to take God some time to turn you around and get you moving in the right direction.

The starting point is for you to be willing to allow God to begin the change. Even after you make a commitment with all of your heart, you're still going to have a self to deal with. You don't get delivered of your self. The only way you can get delivered from your carnal self is to die physically.

VI. To become a living sacrifice, you have to die to yourself and your own selfish ambitions.

  A. A sacrifice is at the mercy of the person doing the sacrificing.

  B. Dying to one's *self* isn't what fallen human beings naturally desire, and the majority of Christians are *still* that way.

  C. Selfishness is how Satan gains access to you.

    i. God had created a perfect world for Adam and Eve, but Satan tempted them to think He was holding something back.

  D. All human beings start out selfish, but they don't have to stay that way.

VII. I was doing all the *right* things for all the *wrong* reasons.

  A. Then, the night of March 23, 1968, God showed me that my heart was all wrong.

  B. I started confessing all of the self-centered things I was seeing about myself—all of the lust and hate that was in my heart, and the way I thought of other people.

  C. I expected God to kill me because of how unrighteous I was, but instead of wrath and rejection, the tangible love of God came over me and changed my life.

  D. I knew it had nothing to do with me—it was solely according to His grace.

VIII. Not everybody is going to have the same kind of dramatic encounter that I did, but everybody needs to have a similar experience—a time when you make the decision to quit sitting on the throne of your life, trying to determine your own future.

  A. Until you reach that place, God can't reveal His perfect will—or He certainly can't reveal the entirety of it—because you would go out and try to do it in your own strength and would end up getting hurt or hurting others.

  B. It will take a period of time for you to be able to learn God's plan and for Him to work some things out in you.

  C. Yielding to the Lord isn't a one-time decision—you have to keep making the choice to surrender.

  D. As long as you are breathing, you have a self, and that carnal nature is going to seek to reassert its desires.

  E. I haven't always loved God flawlessly and avoided all selfishness, but as soon as I see selfishness rise up in my life, I repent—"Father, I'm not going that way. Thank You for showing me."

  F. I committed myself to God in 1968 and have not been uncommitted since.

G. You can reach a place where you literally turn everything over to God, and that's all there is to it—a place where no matter what God tells you to do, you will do it without discussion.

IX. When the Lord first called Jamie and me to go to Pritchett, Colorado, I didn't have any desire to go there, but the moment I was sure God wanted me to do it, I did it.

   A. Once I committed to following God's leading to go to Pritchett, He put His desires in my heart, and I fell in love with the place.

   B. I have discovered that most people aren't like that.

      i. It's one of the reasons God hasn't revealed His will to them yet.

      ii. It's also the reason they are struggling.

X. It solves a lot of problems when you figure out there's only one God—and you aren't Him!

   A. The heart of God's will for you is to be a living sacrifice, committed unto Him.

   B. Once you reach that place, you will have to rebel against God to keep from seeing His good, acceptable, and perfect will come to pass in your life (Rom. 12:2).

   C. Commit your life to Him, and you will prosper and have the favor of God.

   D. God can direct your life better than you can (Jer. 10:23), so don't lean unto your own understanding (Prov. 3:5).

   E. Most people want to skip fully submitting to God and move on up to the top of the ladder—they want to stride right into the center of God's will and see great things happen.

   F. The reason there are people in ministry who wind up committing adultery and stealing money is because they didn't take the time to build a foundation of character and integrity.

   G. Don't make that mistake by trying to get around becoming a living sacrifice.

XI. Most people don't trust God to advance them in life because they're too busy trying to advance themselves.

   A. In general, they demand respect and assert their rights in an attempt to make everyone around them realize how important they are, which is pretty much the opposite of being a living sacrifice.

   B. Being committed to God doesn't mean you lay down like a doormat every time you are confronted with a problem.

C. If God tells you to do something to change your circumstances, you need to do it, but you shouldn't be motivated by selfish desires.

D. If you are living a totally selfish life right now, you have a lot of momentum built up in that direction.

E. It's going to take God some time to turn you around and get you moving in the right direction.

F. The starting point is for you to be willing to allow God to begin the change.

G. Even after you make a commitment with all of your heart, you're still going to have a self to deal with.

H. The only way you can get delivered from your carnal self is to die physically.

6. To become a living sacrifice, you have to die to yourself and your own selfish ambitions. A sacrifice is at the mercy of the person doing the sacrificing. Dying to one's *self* isn't what fallen human beings naturally desire, and the majority of Christians are *still* that way. Selfishness is how Satan gains access to you. God had created a perfect world for Adam and Eve, but Satan tempted them to think He was holding something back. All human beings start out selfish, but they don't have to stay that way.

6a. What do you have to do to become a living sacrifice?
You have to die to yourself and your own selfish ambitions

6b. Discussion question: Why do you think the majority of Christians don't desire dying to self?
Discussion question

6c. How did Satan gain access to Adam and Eve?
By tempting them to think God was holding something back

7. I was doing all the *right* things for all the *wrong* reasons. Then, the night of March 23, 1968, God showed me that my heart was all wrong. I started confessing all of the self-centered things I was seeing about myself—all of the lust and hate that was in my heart, and the way I thought of other people. I expected God to kill me because of how unrighteous I was, but instead of wrath and rejection, the tangible love of God came over me and changed my life. I knew it had me—it was solely according to His grace.

7a. What happened after Andrew confessed all he did to God, and he expected God to kill him?
The tangible love of God came over him and changed his life

7b. True or false: It had nothing to do with Andrew.
True

8. Not everybody is going to have the same kind of dramatic encounter that I did, but everybody needs to have a similar experience—a time when you make the decision to quit sitting on the throne of your life, trying to determine your own future. Until you reach that place, God can't reveal His perfect will—or He certainly can't reveal the entirety of it—because you would go out and try to do it in your own strength and would end up getting hurt or hurting others. It will take a period of time for you to be able to learn God's plan and for Him to work some things out in you. Yielding to the Lord isn't a one-time decision—you have to keep making the choice to surrender. As long as you are breathing, you have a self, and that carnal nature is going to seek to reassert its desires. I haven't always loved God flawlessly and avoided all selfishness, but as soon as I see selfishness rise up in my life, I repent—"Father, I'm not going that way. Thank You for showing me." I committed myself to God in 1968 and have not been uncommitted since. You can reach a place where you literally turn everything over to God, and that's all there is to it—a place where no matter what God tells you to do, you will do it without discussion.

8a. If you're sitting on the throne of your life, trying to determine your own future, what can't God do?
He can't reveal His perfect will—or He certainly can't reveal the entirety of it— because you would go out and try to do it in your own strength and would end up getting hurt or hurting others

8b. True or false: Yielding to the Lord is not a one-time decision.
True

8c. Discussion question: Why do you think the carnal nature seeks to reassert its desires?
Discussion question

8d. What does Andrew do when he sees selfishness rise up in his life?
A. He welcomes it
B. He denies it
C. He repents of it
D. All of the above
E. None of the above
C. He repents of it

8e. You can reach a place where you literally turn everything over to God—a place where no matter what He tells you to do, you will do it without _____.
Discussion

9. When the Lord first called Jamie and me to go to Pritchett, Colorado, I didn't have any desire to go there, but the moment I was sure God wanted me to do it, I did it. Once I committed to following God's leading to go to Pritchett, He put His desires in my heart, and I fell in love with the place. I have discovered that most people aren't like that. It's one of the reasons God hasn't revealed His will to them yet. It's also the reason they are struggling.

9a.   What happened once Andrew committed to following God's leading to go to Pritchett?
  A. God didn't help him
  B. God changed His mind
  C. God criticized him for taking so long
  D. God made him His slave
  E. God put His desires in his heart
  E. God put His desires in his heart

9b.   Discussion question: Why do you think people are struggling who aren't like that?
Discussion question

10. It solves a lot of problems when you figure out there's only one God—and you aren't Him! The heart of God's will for you is to be a living sacrifice, committed unto Him. Once you reach that place, you will have to rebel against God to keep from seeing His good, acceptable, and perfect will come to pass in your life (Rom. 12:2). Commit your life to Him, and you will prosper and have the favor of God. God can direct your life better than you can (Jer. 10:23), so don't lean unto your own understanding (Prov. 3:5). Most people want to skip fully submitting to God and move on up to the top of the ladder—they want to stride right into the center of God's will and see great things happen. The reason there are people in ministry who wind up committing adultery and stealing money is because they didn't take the time to build a foundation of character and integrity. Don't make that mistake by trying to get around becoming a living sacrifice.

10a.   Discussion question: Once you are a living sacrifice, committed to Him, why do you think you would have to rebel against God to keep from seeing His good, acceptable, and perfect will come to pass in your life?
Discussion question

10b.   True or false: People who are committed to God don't necessarily have the favor of God.
False

10c.   Read Jeremiah 10:23 and Proverbs 3:5. Why shouldn't you lean unto your own understanding?
Because God can direct your life better than you can

10d.   Discussion question: What are some reasons becoming a living sacrifice isn't optional?
Discussion question

11. Most people don't trust God to advance them in life because they're too busy trying to advance themselves. In general, they demand respect and assert their rights in an attempt to make everyone around them realize how important they are, which is pretty much the opposite of being a living sacrifice. Being committed to God doesn't mean you lay down like a doormat every time you are confronted with a problem. If God tells you to do something to change your circumstances, you need to do it, but you shouldn't be motivated by selfish desires. If you are living a totally selfish life right now, you have a lot of momentum built up in that direction. It's going to take God some time to turn you around and get you moving in the right direction. The starting point is for you to be willing to allow God to begin the change. Even after you make a commitment with all of your heart, you're still going to have a self to deal with. The only way you can get delivered from your carnal self is to die physically.

11a. Most people don't _____ God to advance them in life because they're too busy trying to advance themselves.
Trust

11b. If you demand respect and assert your rights in an attempt to make everyone around you realize how important you are, what is that?
Pretty much the opposite of being a living sacrifice

11c. True or false: Being committed to God doesn't mean you lay down like a doormat every time you are confronted with a problem.
True

11d. If you are living a totally selfish life right now, why is it going to take God some time to turn you around and get you moving in the right direction?
A. Because God needs to teach you a lesson through it
B. Because you have a lot of momentum built up in that direction
C. Because God wants to take as long as possible
D. All of the above
E. None of the above
B. Because you have a lot of momentum built up in that direction

11e. Even after you make a commitment with all of your heart, you're still going to have a _____ to deal with.
Self

20. What do you have to do to become a living sacrifice?

_____

_____

_____

21. Discussion question: Why do you think the majority of Christians don't desire dying to self?

_____

_____

_____

22. How did Satan gain access to Adam and Eve?

_____

_____

_____

23. What happened after Andrew confessed all he did to God, and he expected God to kill him?

_____

_____

_____

24. True or false: It had nothing to do with Andrew.

25. If you're sitting on the throne of your life, trying to determine your own future, what can't God do?

_____

_____

_____

26. True or false: Yielding to the Lord is not a one-time decision.

27. Discussion question: Why do you think the carnal nature seeks to reassert its desires?

_____

_____

_____

28. What does Andrew do when he sees selfishness rise up in his life?
    A. He welcomes it
    B. He denies it
    C. He repents of it
    D. All of the above
    E. None of the above

29. You can reach a place where you literally turn everything over to God—a place where no matter what He tells you to do, you will do it without _____.

30. What happened once Andrew committed to following God's leading to go to Pritchett?
    A. God didn't help him
    B. God changed His mind
    C. God criticized him for taking so long
    D. God made him His slave
    E. God put His desires in his heart

31. Discussion question: Why do you think people are struggling who aren't like that?

_____

_____

_____

32. Discussion question: Once you are a living sacrifice, committed to Him, why do you think you would have to rebel against God to keep from seeing His good, acceptable, and perfect will come to pass in your life?

_____

_____

_____

33. True or false: People who are committed to God don't necessarily have the favor of God.

34. Read Jeremiah 10:23 and Proverbs 3:5. Why shouldn't you lean unto your own understanding?

_____

_____

_____

35. Discussion question: What are some reasons becoming a living sacrifice isn't optional?

_____

_____

_____

36. Most people don't _____ God to advance them in life because they're too busy trying to advance themselves.

37. If you demand respect and assert your rights in an attempt to make everyone around you realize how important you are, what is that?

_____

_____

_____

38. True or false: Being committed to God doesn't mean you lay down like a doormat every time you are confronted with a problem.

39. If you are living a totally selfish life right now, why is it going to take God some time to turn you around and get you moving in the right direction?
    A. Because God needs to teach you a lesson through it
    B. Because you have a lot of momentum built up in that direction
    C. Because God wants to take as long as possible
    D. All of the above
    E. None of the above

40. Even after you make a commitment with all of your heart, you're still going to have a _____ to deal with.

20. You have to die to yourself and your own selfish ambitions
21. *Discussion question*
22. By tempting them to think God was holding something back
23. The tangible love of God came over him and changed his life
24. True
25. He can't reveal His perfect will—or He certainly can't reveal the entirety of it—because you would go out and try to do it in your own strength and would end up getting hurt or hurting others
26. True
27. *Discussion question*
28. C. He repents of it
29. Discussion
30. E. God put His desires in his heart
31. *Discussion question*
32. *Discussion question*
33. False
34. Because God can direct your life better than you can
35. *Discussion question*
36. Trust
37. Pretty much the opposite of being a living sacrifice
38. True
39. B. Because you have a lot of momentum built up in that direction
40. Self

ROMANS 12:2

And be not conformed to this world: but be ye transformed by the renewing of your mind, that ye may prove what is that good, and acceptable, and perfect, will of God.

JEREMIAH 10:23

O Lord, I know that the way of man is not in himself: it is not in man that walketh to direct his steps.

PROVERBS 3:5

Trust in the Lord with all thine heart; and lean not unto thine own understanding.

LESSON 3.3

Jim Erwin was one of the astronauts who walked on the moon. I was in Vietnam when all of that was going on, but I always wanted to know more about it. One day, I was on a television program with Jim and had the opportunity to talk to him about the lunar landing. I thought the technology was so awesome—blasting off for the moon and landing on the exact spot they were aiming for.

But as I talked to Jim, I learned it wasn't like that at all. He said that NASA basically threw the capsule toward the moon and every ten minutes for four days, they had to adjust their direction in order to stay on course. Sometimes the capsule was ninety degrees off from the direction it needed to be traveling, so they had to fire up the rocket to get back on track. Other times they were just a fraction of an inch off.

The flight path to the moon wasn't a straight line; it was a jumble of zigzags. Jim said they had a 500-mile-long target area for their landing. When he got out of the lunar module and stepped onto the moon, he was within five feet of being outside the landing zone. They nearly missed a 500-mile landing strip! But they still made it.

As Jim was telling me this, the Lord spoke to me and said, "That's the way it is when you make a commitment of your life to God." It's not like you commit once and never make another mistake or mess up. You make a total commitment, and within five or ten minutes, you are going to have an opportunity for a course correction. Somebody is going to cut in front of you in line at the grocery store, cut you off in traffic, or say something rude. You will have the opportunity to make a course correction every ten minutes for the rest of your life!

The problem with a living sacrifice is that it keeps trying to crawl off the altar. You need to make a total commitment. Don't be surprised if you wake up one morning thinking, *What about me? What about my desires and ambitions?* It doesn't mean you weren't committed to God or that you won't make it. It just means that you still have "flesh" that needs to be subdued. Just deny your flesh and make a course correction.

You will experience the beginning of God when you come to the end of yourself, which isn't to say that you can't encounter God every once in a while or that He can't touch you. God loves you, and He will move in your life as much as you let Him. But you aren't going to see the miraculous power of God consistently working in your life until you quit trying to do everything yourself, and put Him first.

Everyone is totally self-centered when they come out of the womb. If you have never taken the step of putting God first, you are *still* self-centered. You might be a twenty-, thirty-, forty-, or sixty-year-old adult brat who still thinks that life is all about *you.* You've heard the joke about how many people it takes to change a light bulb, right? In most cases, the answer is "just one," because the person holds the bulb, and the world revolves around them—*or at least that's what they think.*

God created us to live for a greater purpose than just satisfying our own needs. We need to humble ourselves and make ourselves living sacrifices. That's not all there is to fulfilling God's will, but you can't do anything else until you take this first step. Some people make a total commitment to God and then get off course. If you made a total commitment to God in the past, then maybe He is just trying to tell you, "Hey, you're off track." No big deal; just make a course correction and get back to the commitment you have already made to follow God.

The vast majority of people who are searching for God's will have probably never turned control of their lives over to the Lord. If you're thinking, *I'm an adult brat. I'm totally self-centered. My whole life has been about me,* then you need to make a commitment to God. Allow God to give you guidance about the direction to take with your future. If there is any doubt in your mind about whether or not you have made a total commitment to God, then you haven't done it. If you are feeling a tug on your heart to make a commitment, I suggest you respond now while the Holy Spirit is leading you.

Becoming a living sacrifice isn't only for the "super-saints" or those who *really* want to seek God; every born-again believer is supposed to be a living sacrifice. Sadly, a lot of our churches are promoting "self-help" philosophies as the way to happiness. But the Christian life isn't about having a positive self-image; it's the Christ-image in us that matters. We need to exalt Christ, not self.

If you are willing to say, "*I need to become a living sacrifice*"—if you are willing to start moving in that direction and want to give God the right to start running your life—you can make that commitment right now. Thank God for showing you the next step. Acknowledge that you are not capable of dying to yourself in your own strength. Determine to become a living sacrifice and trust the Lord to start leading you out of selfishness and into His plans for your life. Give God the freedom to show you the way you should go and then resolve to follow His leading.

I believe that as you humble yourself under the mighty hand of God, He will lift you up (1 Pet. 5:6). As you turn your life over to Him, He will begin a process of renewal. This step you are taking is not merely a mental acknowledgement of God's supremacy; it's a supernatural restoration process through which Jesus will begin to dominate your focus. The moment you make this decision, you will begin to recognize how God is moving in your life to bless you and give you direction. I believe that as you turn your life over to God, He will touch your heart, and you will never be the same.

OUTLINE • 3.3

XII. It's not like you commit once and never make another mistake or mess up.

   A. You make a total commitment, and within five or ten minutes, you are going to have an opportunity for a course correction.

      i. Somebody is going to cut in front of you in line at the grocery store, cut you off in traffic, or say something rude.

   B. The problem with a living sacrifice is that it keeps trying to crawl off the altar.

   C. It doesn't mean you weren't committed to God or that you won't make it; it just means that you still have "flesh" that needs to be subdued.

   D. Just deny your flesh and make a course correction.

XIII. You will experience the beginning of God when you come to the end of yourself.

   A. This isn't to say that you can't encounter God every once in a while or that He can't touch you.

   B. God loves you, and He will move in your life as much as you let Him.

   C. But you aren't going to see the miraculous power of God consistently working in your life until you quit trying to do everything yourself, and put Him first.

   D. Everyone is totally self-centered when they come out of the womb, and if you have never taken the step of putting God first, you are *still* self-centered.

XIV. God created you to live for a greater purpose than just satisfying your own needs.

   A. Being a living sacrifice is not all there is to fulfilling God's will, but you can't do anything else until you take this first step.

   B. If you made a total commitment to God but have gotten off course, just make a course correction and get back to the commitment you have already made to follow God.

   C. The vast majority of people who are searching for God's will have probably never turned control of their lives over to the Lord.

   D. Allow God to give you guidance about the direction to take with your future.

   E. If you are feeling a tug on your heart to make a commitment, I suggest you respond now while the Holy Spirit is leading you.

XV. Becoming a living sacrifice isn't only for the "super-saints" or those who *really* want to seek God.

   A. Every born-again believer is supposed to be a living sacrifice.

B. The Christian life isn't about having a positive self-image; it's the Christ-image in you that matters.

C. Acknowledge that you are not capable of dying to yourself in your own strength.

D. Trust the Lord to start leading you out of selfishness and into His plans for your life.

E. Give God the freedom to show you the way you should go and then resolve to follow His leading.

XVI. I believe that as you humble yourself under the mighty hand of God, He will lift you up (1 Pet. 5:6).

A. As you turn your life over to Him, He will begin a process of renewal.

B. This step you are taking is not merely a mental acknowledgement of God's supremacy; it's a supernatural restoration process through which Jesus will begin to dominate your focus.

C. The moment you make this decision, you will begin to recognize how God is moving in your life to bless you and give you direction.

D. I believe that as you turn your life over to God, He will touch your heart, and you will never be the same.

12. It's not like you commit once and never make another mistake or mess up. You make a total commitment, and within five or ten minutes, you are going to have an opportunity for a course correction. Somebody is going to cut in front of you in line at the grocery store, cut you off in traffic, or say something rude. The problem with a living sacrifice is that it keeps trying to crawl off the altar. It doesn't mean you weren't committed to God or that you won't make it; it just means that you still have "flesh" that needs to be subdued. Just deny your flesh and make a course correction.

12a. True or false: You commit once and never make another mistake or mess up.
False

12b. Why does a living sacrifice keep trying to crawl off the altar?
    A. Because that's the way God designed it
    B. Because a living sacrifice doesn't know any better
    C. Because no one said it shouldn't
    D. Because flesh has not been subdued
    E. Because it wasn't the best time
    D. Because flesh has not been subdued

12c. You need to deny your flesh and make a what?
Course correction

13. You will experience the beginning of God when you come to the end of yourself. This isn't to say that you can't encounter God every once in a while or that He can't touch you. God loves you, and He will move in your life as much as you let Him. But you aren't going to see the miraculous power of God consistently working in your life until you quit trying to do everything yourself, and put Him first. Everyone is totally self-centered when they come out of the womb, and if you have never taken the step of putting God first, you are *still* self-centered.

13a. Discussion question: How have you experienced the beginning of God when you came to the end of yourself?
Discussion question

13b. God loves you, and He will move in your life as much as you _____ Him.
Let

13c. You need to take the step of putting God first if you don't want to be what?
    A. Selfless
    B. Holy
    C. Self-centered
    D. All of the above
    E. None of the above
    C. Self-centered

14. God created you to live for a greater purpose than just satisfying your own needs. Being a living sacrifice is not all there is to fulfilling God's will, but you can't do anything else until you take this first step. If you made a total commitment to God but have gotten off course, just make a course correction and get back to the commitment you have already made to follow God. The vast majority of people who are searching for God's will have probably never turned control of their lives over to the Lord. Allow God to give you guidance about the direction to take with your future. If you are feeling a tug on your heart to make a commitment, I suggest you respond now while the Holy Spirit is leading you.

14a. Being a living sacrifice is not all there is to fulfilling God's will, but what can't you until do until you take this first step?
Anything else

14b. If you made a total commitment to God but have gotten off course, what do you need to do?
Make a course correction and get back to the commitment you have already made to follow God

14c. Discussion question: Why do you think the vast majority of people who are searching for God's will have probably never turned control of their lives over to the Lord?
Discussion question

14b. If you are feeling a tug on your heart to make a commitment, what does Andrew suggest?
   A. That you respond now while the Holy Spirit is leading you
   B. That you consult your church leader before you do anything
   C. That you make sure no one knows what you're about to do
   D. That you take an entire day or more to think about it
   E. That you save up enough money to do so
   A. That you respond now while the Holy Spirit is leading you

15. Becoming a living sacrifice isn't only for the "super-saints" or those who *really* want to seek God. Every born-again believer is supposed to be a living sacrifice. The Christian life isn't about having a positive self-image; it's the Christ-image in you that matters. Acknowledge that you are not capable of dying to yourself in your own strength. Trust the Lord to start leading you out of selfishness and into His plans for your life. Give God the freedom to show you the way you should go and then resolve to follow His leading.

15a. True or false: Every born-again believer is supposed to be a living sacrifice.
True

15b. What matters in the Christian life?
The Christ-image in you

15c. What should you acknowledge?
That you are not capable of dying to yourself in your own strength

15d. Therefore, what should you do?
  A. Trust the Lord to start leading you out of selfishness and into His plans for your life
  B. Trust a psychologist to start leading you out of selfishness and into His plans for your life
  C. Don't trust anyone to start leading you out of selfishness and into His plans for your life
  D. All of the above
  E. None of the above
  A. Trust the Lord to start leading you out of selfishness and into His plans for your life

15e. _____ to follow His leading.
Resolve

16. I believe that as you humble yourself under the mighty hand of God, He will lift you up (1 Pet. 5:6). As you turn your life over to Him, He will begin a process of renewal. This step you are taking is not merely a mental acknowledgement of God's supremacy; it's a supernatural restoration process through which Jesus will begin to dominate your focus. The moment you make this decision, you will begin to recognize how God is moving in your life to bless you and give you direction. I believe that as you turn your life over to God, He will touch your heart, and you will never be the same.

16a. Read 1 Peter 5:6. Humble yourself under the mighty hand of God, and He will _____ you up.
Lift

16b. This step you are taking is not merely a mental acknowledgement of God's supremacy, but what else is it?
A supernatural restoration process through which Jesus will begin to dominate your focus

16c. Discussion question: How has God moved in your life to bless you and give you direction?
Discussion question

16d. What will happen as you turn your life over to God?
He will touch your heart, and you will never be the same

41. True or false: You commit once and never make another mistake or mess up.

42. Why does a living sacrifice keep trying to crawl off the altar?
    A. Because that's the way God designed it
    B. Because a living sacrifice doesn't know any better
    C. Because no one said it shouldn't
    D. Because flesh has not been subdued
    E. Because it wasn't the best time

43. You need to deny your flesh and make a what?

    _____

    _____

    _____

44. Discussion question: How have you experienced the beginning of God when you came to the end of yourself?

    _____

    _____

    _____

45. God loves you, and He will move in your life as much as you _____ Him.

46. You need to take the step of putting God first if you don't want to be what?
    A. Selfless
    B. Holy
    C. Self-centered
    D. All of the above
    E. None of the above

47. Being a living sacrifice is not all there is to fulfilling God's will, but what can't you until do until you take this first step?

    _____

    _____

    _____

48. If you made a total commitment to God but have gotten off course, what do you need to do?

_____

_____

_____

49. Discussion question: Why do you think the vast majority of people who are searching for God's will have probably never turned control of their lives over to the Lord?

_____

_____

_____

50. If you are feeling a tug on your heart to make a commitment, what does Andrew suggest?
    A. That you respond now while the Holy Spirit is leading you
    B. That you consult your church leader before you do anything
    C. That you make sure no one knows what you're about to do
    D. That you take an entire day or more to think about it
    E. That you save up enough money to do so

51. True or false: Every born-again believer is supposed to be a living sacrifice.

52. What matters in the Christian life?

_____

_____

_____

53. What should you acknowledge?

_____

_____

_____

54. Therefore, what should you do?
    A. Trust the Lord to start leading you out of selfishness and into His plans for your life
    B. Trust a psychologist to start leading you out of selfishness and into His plans for your life
    C. Don't trust anyone to start leading you out of selfishness and into His plans for your life
    D. All of the above
    E. None of the above

55. _____ to follow His leading.

56. Read 1 Peter 5:6. Humble yourself under the mighty hand of God, and He will
_____ you up.

57. This step you are taking is not merely a mental acknowledgement of God's supremacy, but what else is it?

_____

_____

_____

58. Discussion question: How has God moved in your life to bless you and give you direction?

_____

_____

_____

59. What will happen as you turn your life over to God?

_____

_____

_____

41. False
42. D. Because flesh has not been subdued
43. Course correction
44. *Discussion question*
45. Let
46. C. Self-centered
47. Anything else
48. Make a course correction and get back to the commitment you have already made to follow God
49. *Discussion question*
50. A. That you respond now while the Holy Spirit is leading you
51. True
52. The Christ-image in you
53. That you are not capable of dying to yourself in your own strength
54. A. Trust the Lord to start leading you out of selfishness and into His plans for your life
55. Resolve
56. Lift
57. A supernatural restoration process through which Jesus will begin to dominate your focus
58. *Discussion question*
59. He will touch your heart, and you will never be the same

1 PETER 5:6

Humble yourselves therefore under the mighty hand of God, that he may exalt you in due time.

RENEWING YOUR MIND

LESSON 4.1

Becoming a living sacrifice is important, but having a renewed mind is equally important. Without a renewed mind, you will end up missing God's perfect will for your life. A commitment to go anywhere and do anything for God can leave you vulnerable to the devil's manipulation, unless you balance your commitment with knowledge of the truth in God's Word.

At the time God told me to quit school and I ended up being sent to Vietnam, I had some wrong ideas about the true nature of God. When I was growing up, it had been instilled in me by the church I attended that nothing could happen unless God allowed it to, so I thought that whatever happens in life must be God's will. I didn't understand that we have an Enemy and that God isn't the source of the evil in our world. While I was in Vietnam, I spent a lot of time studying the Word, but I still didn't learn the truth that God doesn't tempt people with evil and that He's only the source of good (James 1:13 and 17).

Right after I came home from Vietnam, a traveling minister who had seven incurable diseases came to preach at our church. While he was there, he went to a doctor friend of mine who ran an EKG on him and sent it to the lab for analysis. The lab came back and said, "Is this a joke? You sent us an EKG on a dead guy!"

This minister had seven diseases and an EKG reading that showed he was dead, yet he was alive and preaching at our church. Granted, he was just barely alive. He was struggling. He couldn't stand on his feet, so he just sat in a chair and preached for an hour or two. The basic message he preached was that Satan is God's messenger boy. He was saying that Satan couldn't do anything unless God allowed it; therefore, if you had a problem, God allowed it in your life to teach you something and help you grow.

At that time, I was committed to God and ready to do anything. And here's a guy with seven incurable diseases preaching that God uses Satan to teach us things. As I was listening to him, I started thinking, *Uh oh, what if God wants to teach me something?* Jamie and I were engaged, so during the week this traveling preacher was at our church, I went to the doctor to get a routine exam for our marriage license. The exam revealed that I had jaundice. The doctor said, "If you don't lay flat on your back for a month, you could get really sick." He told me that physical exertion could kill me or put me in a coma. But I determined I wasn't going to lie on my back for a month. I was trying to believe God for healing.

After I learned about my health problem, this traveling minister took me and twelve or fifteen other people from the church out to eat. We were all sitting together, and during the meal, he started to prophesy over me. He said, "You're going to go into a coma. You'll be in a coma for eight years." He went on to talk about how God was putting me into a coma to make me holy, and when I came out, I would be like the Apostle Paul because God would have shown me great revelations. He said that God was going to judge me and do all of this to break me.

I was in tears as I listened to him speak all of that death and destruction over me. I had made a total commitment to God, so I thought, *Well, if this is God's will, I accept it.* I believed everything that preacher was saying. The devil had me convinced that God was going to use sickness to teach me a lesson—but he went too far. If he would have quit right there, you never would have heard of me. I probably would have gone into that coma and died.

He had me on the ropes, but he just wouldn't quit. The preacher kept pouring it on. He kept talking about how terrible all of the suffering was on him, and finally he said, "The worst thing about this is that God has put me on a fast from the Bible for eight years. He told me that for eight years, I can't read the Word. The only time I open the Bible is when I preach to other people." When he said that, it grabbed my attention. I didn't know a lot back then, but I knew better than to believe that God would tell someone not to read the Bible.

I was in love with God and excited about the Word. I had just come home from Vietnam—where I had spent the majority of every day reading the Bible. God's Word was my meditation day and night. The minute that preacher said those things, I stood up and said, "I reject this in the name of Jesus. I am not accepting this stuff. I don't understand everything, but I know God would never put me on a fast from the Word of God." Jamie and I left that church, we left our closest friends, and we walked away from that teaching. Praise God, my mind was renewed to just enough truth to recognize that he was preaching a lie.

You need to be a living sacrifice. If you don't renew your mind to the truth, Satan will take advantage of your desire to do anything for God. You need to balance your commitment to the Lord with a revelation of Truth that comes from His Word. Jamie and I avoided a disaster because we had renewed our minds just enough to know God would never tell us not to read His Word. But what would have happened if we didn't know that truth? I don't have to imagine. I have a perfect example.

Two years earlier, I heard this same minister teach the same things. I brought his teaching entitled, "Satan Is God's Messenger Boy" home and gave it to my girlfriend. She happened to also be one of Jamie's best friends and loved God with all of her heart. She had also made a commitment to be a living sacrifice to the Lord.

In his teaching, the minister used an example of a boy who wanted to be a witness for the Lord but was shy and introverted. He found it hard to witness to his football buddies, so he prayed and asked the Lord to give him an incurable disease so he could show them he wasn't afraid of death. Sure enough, at his funeral, four of his football teammates were born again because of his testimony.

As a result of listening to this teaching, my girlfriend prayed a similar prayer, and the next morning, she had to be rushed to the hospital. She was diagnosed with acute leukemia and believed the Lord had given this to her as an answer to her prayer—in order to break her and glorify Himself. I had gone off to Vietnam during this time, and although we were only officially boyfriend and girlfriend, her parents said we were engaged and got me an emergency leave to come home and be with her during her final days.

I was with her when she hemorrhaged and strangled to death on her own blood. It was devastating, but at the time, we thought this was God's will. Sure enough, at her funeral, four people gave their lives to the Lord. Of course, I now know God didn't do this, nor did He allow it. We allowed it because of our wrong beliefs. The Lord used this situation to bring some people to Himself, but He didn't cause it. Satan used this to hurt a number of people, who are still reeling from it today. Our hearts may have been good, but our minds were wrong. This demonstrates how being a living sacrifice can be dangerous if we don't have our minds renewed with the truth of God's Word.

You Choose the Mold

And be not conformed to this world: but be ye transformed by the renewing of your mind, that ye may prove what is that good, and acceptable, and perfect, will of God.

ROMANS 12:2

The Greek word that was translated *"conformed"* in this verse means to pour into a mold. As Christians, we shouldn't be poured into the mold of this world. This reminds me of when I was drafted into the Army and received orders to go to Vietnam. I was sitting in a room along with everyone else who had been drafted at the same time. The officials came in and told us we were going to war, and a lot of the guys started crying. So, they called in a chaplain, and he said, "The Army is a fire, and it will melt you. But you get to pick what mold you fit into."

I realized right then that I wasn't going to come out of the Army the same man I was when I went in. The experience was going to melt me, but I was going to pick the mold. I was going to choose to be conformed to the image of Jesus. I took that chaplain's message to heart and came out of the Army ten times stronger in the Lord than I was when I went in.

In the same way, the experiences of life are going to melt you. You aren't going to leave this world with the same mentality you had when you came into it. Life is going to test you. You are going to be melted. But you get to pick the mold you get squeezed into. As a Christian, you need to be changed into the image of Christ.

The way to keep from being conformed to the image of this world is through the renewing of your mind. The Scripture says, *"Be ye transformed by the renewing of your mind."* The Greek word for *"transformed"* in that passage is *metamorphoō*, which comes from the same word we get "metamorphosis" from—the process of a caterpillar spinning a cocoon and emerging a little while later as a butterfly. It's a word picture for your life. If you want to change from something that is earthbound to something that is flying and beautiful—if you want *metamorphosis*—you have to renew your mind.

OUTLINE • 4.1

I. Becoming a living sacrifice is important, but having a renewed mind is equally important.

    A. Without a renewed mind, you will end up missing God's perfect will for your life.

    B. A commitment to go anywhere and do anything for God can leave you vulnerable to the devil's manipulation, unless you balance your commitment with knowledge of the truth in God's Word.

    C. When I was growing up, it had been instilled in me that nothing could happen unless God allowed it to, so I thought that whatever happens in life must be God's will.

    D. I spent a lot of time studying the Word, but I still didn't learn the truth that God doesn't tempt people with evil and that He's only the source of good (James 1:13 and 17).

II. A traveling minister preached at our church that Satan couldn't do anything unless God allowed it; therefore, if you had a problem, God allowed it in your life to teach you something and help you grow.

    A. He began to prophesy over me that I would be in a coma for eight years to make me holy, and when I came out, I would be like the Apostle Paul because God would have shown me great revelations.

    B. I believed everything that preacher was saying—the devil had me convinced that God was going to use sickness to teach me a lesson—but the devil went too far when the preacher told me that for eight years, I couldn't read the Word.

    C. I stood up and said, "I reject this in the name of Jesus. I don't understand everything, but I know God would never put me on a fast from the Word of God."

    D. Praise God, my mind was renewed to just enough truth to recognize that he was preaching a lie.

    E. You need to be a living sacrifice, but if you don't renew your mind to the truth, Satan will take advantage of your desire to do anything for God.

    F. You need to balance your commitment to the Lord with a revelation of Truth that comes from His Word.

    G. Being a living sacrifice can be dangerous if you don't have your mind renewed with the truth of God's Word.

III. The Greek word that was translated "*conformed*" in Romans 12:2 means to pour into a mold.

    A. The experiences of life are going to melt you—you aren't going to leave this world with the same mentality you had when you came into it.

    B. Life is going to test you, but you get to pick the mold you get squeezed into.

    C. You need to be changed into the image of Christ.

IV. The way to keep from being conformed to the image of this world is through the renewing of your mind.

    A. The Scripture says, *"Be ye transformed by the renewing of your mind."*

    B. The Greek word for *"transformed"* in that passage is *metamorphoō,* which comes from the same word we get "metamorphosis" from—the process of a caterpillar spinning a cocoon and emerging a little while later as a butterfly.

    C. It's a word picture for your life: If you want to change from something that is earthbound to something that is flying and beautiful—if you want *metamorphosis*—you have to renew your mind.

1. Becoming a living sacrifice is important, but having a renewed mind is equally important. Without a renewed mind, you will end up missing God's perfect will for your life. A commitment to go anywhere and do anything for God can leave you vulnerable to the devil's manipulation, unless you balance your commitment with knowledge of the truth in God's Word. When I was growing up, it had been instilled in me that nothing could happen unless God allowed it to, so I thought that whatever happens in life must be God's will. I spent a lot of time studying the Word, but I still didn't learn the truth that God doesn't tempt people with evil and that He's only the source of good (James 1:13 and 17).

1a.   Why is having a renewed mind as equally important as being a living sacrifice?
Because unless you balance your commitment with knowledge of the truth in God's Word, you are vulnerable to the devil's manipulation

1b.   Read James 1:13 and 17. God is doesn't tempt people with evil, and He's only the _____ of good.
Source

2. A traveling minister preached at our church that Satan couldn't do anything unless God allowed it; therefore, if you had a problem, God allowed it in your life to teach you something and help you grow. He began to prophesy over me that I would be in a coma for eight years to make me holy, and when I came out, I would be like the Apostle Paul because God would have shown me great revelations. I believed everything that preacher was saying—the devil had me convinced that God was going to use sickness to teach me a lesson—but the devil went too far when the preacher told me that for eight years, I couldn't read the Word. I stood up and said, "I reject this in the name of Jesus. I don't understand everything, but I know God would never put me on a fast from the Word of God." Praise God, my mind was renewed to just enough truth to recognize that he was preaching a lie. You need to be a living sacrifice, but if you don't renew your mind to the truth, Satan will take advantage of your desire to do anything for God. You need to balance your commitment to the Lord with a revelation of Truth that comes from His Word. Being a living sacrifice can be dangerous if you don't have your mind renewed with the truth of God's Word.

2a.   Discussion question: The fact that the devil went too far, what does it say about him?
Discussion question

2b.   When your mind is renewed to the truth, what will you reject?
A. A lie
B. Dessert
C. Teachers
D. All of the above
E. None of the above
A. A lie

2c.   What do you need to balance your commitment with?
A revelation of Truth that comes from God's Word

3. The Greek word that was translated *"conformed"* in Romans 12:2 means to pour into a mold. The experiences of life are going to melt you—you aren't going to leave this world with the same mentality you had when you came into it. Life is going to test you, but you get to pick the mold you get squeezed into. You need to be changed into the image of Christ.

3a. Discussion question: In your own words, what does *"conformed"* mean?
Discussion question

3b. True or false: You aren't going to leave this world with the same mentality you had when you came into it.
True

3c. What do you get to pick?
The mold you get squeezed into

3d. You need to be changed into the _____ of Christ.
Image

4. The way to keep from being conformed to the image of this world is through the renewing of your mind. The Scripture says, *"Be ye transformed by the renewing of your mind."* The Greek word for *"transformed"* in that passage is *metamorphoō*, which comes from the same word we get "metamorphosis" from—the process of a caterpillar spinning a cocoon and emerging a little while later as a butterfly. It's a word picture for your life: If you want to change from something that is earthbound to something that is flying and beautiful—if you want *metamorphosis*—you have to renew your mind.

4a. How do you keep from being conformed to the image of this world?
Through the renewing of your mind

4b. Discussion question: Why do you think the metamorphosis of a caterpillar into a butterfly is a picture for your life?
Discussion question

4c. You have to renew your mind if you want what?
A. Power
B. God's love
C. Trust
D. To avoid late fees
E. Metamorphosis
E. Metamorphosis

DISCIPLESHIP QUESTIONS • 4.1

1. Why is having a renewed mind as equally important as being a living sacrifice?

   _____

   _____

   _____

2. Read James 1:13 and 17. God is doesn't tempt people with evil, and He's only the
   _____ of good.

3. Discussion question: The fact that the devil went too far, what does it say about him?

   _____

   _____

   _____

4. When your mind is renewed to the truth, what will you reject?
   A. A lie
   B. Dessert
   C. Teachers
   D. All of the above
   E. None of the above

5. What do you need to balance your commitment with?

   _____

   _____

   _____

6. Discussion question: In your own words, what does *"conformed"* mean?

   _____

   _____

   _____

7. True or false: You aren't going to leave this world with the same mentality you had when
   you came into it.

8. What do you get to pick?

_____

_____

_____

9. You need to be changed into the _____ of Christ.

10. How do you keep from being conformed to the image of this world?

_____

_____

_____

11. Discussion question: Why do you think the metamorphosis of a caterpillar into a butterfly is a picture for your life?

_____

_____

_____

12. You have to renew your mind if you want what?
    A. Power
    B. God's love
    C. Trust
    D. To avoid late fees
    E. Metamorphosis

ANSWER KEY • 4.1

1. Because unless you balance your commitment with knowledge of the truth in God's Word, you are vulnerable to the devil's manipulation
2. Source
3. *Discussion question*
4. A. A lie
5. A revelation of Truth that comes from God's Word
6. *Discussion question*
7. True
8. The mold you get squeezed into
9. Image
10. Through the renewing of your mind
11. *Discussion question*
12. E. Metamorphosis

SCRIPTURES • 4.1

JAMES 1:13
Let no man say when he is tempted, I am tempted of God: for God cannot be tempted with evil, neither tempteth he any man.

JAMES 1:17
Every good gift and every perfect gift is from above, and cometh down from the Father of lights, with whom is no variableness, neither shadow of turning.

ROMANS 12:2
And be not conformed to this world: but be ye transformed by the renewing of your mind, that ye may prove what is that good, and acceptable, and perfect, will of God.

LESSON 4.2

This is so simple that you have to have somebody help you to misunderstand it—yet a lot of the church is missing this point. Most people are praying, "O God, please change everything. Please help my finances. Help my marriage to work out." People know that God can do anything, so they ask Him to rearrange their entire lives in an instant. But not everything happens by prayer alone. I'm not discounting prayer. I believe in the power of prayer. I'm just saying that Scripture says we are born again by the incorruptible seed of God's Word (1 Pet. 1:23). Jesus taught that the sower sows the Word. He also told His disciples that unless they understood that simple principle, they wouldn't understand any of His parables (Mark 4:13-14).

The world we live in operates on the cycle of seeds giving birth to new growth that matures until it can also reproduce by seed. Everything in nature comes from a seed: Plants, animals, and people are all born of a seed. Jesus taught that the kingdom of God also operates like a seed (Matt. 13:31). The seed you have to plant to get kingdom results is the Word of God (Luke 8:11). If you want to have prayers that are regularly answered, you have to sow the Word. The Word of God shows you God's way of thinking. It renews your mind and tears down the obstacles that prevent you from freely receiving all that Christ has already purchased for you.

When people come to me for healing prayer, I often ask them, "What are you doing in response to this sickness?" Typically they will say they have gone to the doctor, taken medication, and prayed. But what I really want to know is, what are they basing their faith on? What seeds have they sown? What scriptures have they used to renew their minds to God's truth? It seems like not one person in a hundred mentions the Word of God. So, I'll say, "What scripture are you basing your faith on?" Usually I get a response like, "Well, I think it says someplace that by Jesus' stripes, we're healed—I think. Isn't that what it says?" Such a limited understanding of God's Word won't get you far.

The Scripture says that by renewing your mind, you are transformed—changed from a creepy crawly thing to something beautiful that can fly. The majority of believers aren't renewing their minds. Most people let their minds be polluted by focusing on what's happening in the world. Consequently, they get squeezed into the mold of the world.

On September 11, 2001, after the terrorist attacks happened, there were Christians who wouldn't fly, because they were just as afraid as the unbelievers. Fear struck their hearts—when the Bible says very clearly to let not your heart be troubled (John 14:1). The psalmist wrote,

> *God is our refuge and strength, a very present help in trouble. [25] Therefore will not we fear, though the earth be removed, and though the mountains be carried into the midst of the sea.*
>
> PSALM 46:1-2

This is saying that if all of the seas covered the earth, we will not be fearful. This is how the Word of God tells us to react. Yet whenever disaster strikes, Christians get into the same fear as unbelievers because they are poured into the mold of this world, instead of having their minds renewed by the Word of God and being poured into His image.

Meditating on the Word will make us think differently than the world. We won't be squeezed into the same mold. We will begin to see things differently and have a different attitude. Christians ought to be different than unbelievers. We shouldn't have the same fear-based reactions as people who don't know Jesus. We are spiritually alive; they are spiritually dead—that's a big difference. The difference between a live person and a dead person should be clear for all to see.

If all the Christians in America were arrested, there wouldn't be enough evidence of their beliefs to convict most of them in a court of law. Believers are just as sick and poor as their neighbors who don't know God. When the layoffs come, Christians are just as afraid of what's going to happen as unbelievers. I'm not saying this to make anyone feel condemned or unworthy. I'm just trying to point out that we have been squeezed into the mold of this world. But we should be a lot different than unbelievers. The reason we aren't different is because we haven't transformed ourselves by the renewing of our minds. We watch *As the Stomach Turns* on television and adopt the world's way of thinking as truth, instead of adopting God's way of thinking.

The Truth Will Set You Free

> *And ye shall know the truth, and the truth shall make you free.*
>
> JOHN 8:32

Jesus said that the Word of God is the truth (John 17:17). The truth is what sets you free—and it's only the truth you *know* that sets you free. You can't just keep the Bible under your arm or on your bedside table and say, "Oh, I believe the Bible." You have to read it and know what it says.

At Charis Bible College, we have a reading program in which our students read the Bible through in one year. Every year some students complain about that, so I tell them, "This is a *Bible* college. I think you should at least read the Bible by the time you graduate." The majority of people who come to the Bible school have probably never read the entire Bible, yet most of them say they believe it.

A lot of people are worried that the Word will lose its freshness or that it will become boring like a novel if they read it all—but that will never happen. I've read through the Bible hundreds of times, and I get more out of it every time I read it. It almost seems like you have to spend thirty years in the Bible just to learn enough to ask the right questions. I'm just now beginning to understand the Word in ways I never have before. So, even if you have read the Bible once, I guarantee that you didn't get it all. You need to be studying the Word and renewing your mind with it on a daily basis.

Many people come to me and say, "I'm powerless. I can't do anything. Would you please pray for me?" But I don't have any special power that they don't have. God has given every born-again believer the same authority. Once you recognize who you are in Christ, you can take your authority, speak to your body, and command sickness to leave. The Bible says, *"Resist the devil, and he will flee from you"* (James 4:7). Many Christians don't realize what God has *already* done for them, so they go to God like a beggar—pleading for an answer to prayer. You need to get rid of that *stinking thinking* because it's killing you.

If Jesus was here in His physical body today, He would not be pleased with our inability. In the Gospel of Matthew, chapter 17, Jesus' disciples brought a man to Him because they had been unable to cast a demon out of the man's son. Jesus didn't say to them, "Oh, don't feel bad about yourselves. It's My fault. I shouldn't have left you alone." No, Jesus called them a faithless and perverse group of people and said, *"How long shall I be with you? how long shall I suffer you? bring him hither to me"* (Matt. 17:17).

This incident occurred before Jesus had died and risen again—before anyone could be born again and become a temple of the Holy Spirit. At the time of that story, the disciples didn't have the advantages we have: We have born-again spirits, we are empowered by the Holy Spirit to do the works that Jesus did, and we have the truth of God's Word at our fingertips. Yet the sick people who come to us for healing aren't always being delivered to the degree that they should be. Jesus told us to meet the needs of people, but we aren't even coming close.

As You Think, So You Are

For as he thinketh in his heart, so is he.

PROVERBS 23:7

Transformation comes by renewing the mind, so in order to experience positive changes in our lives, we need to change the way we think. That's what I mean by getting rid of *stinking thinking*. Our lives go in the direction of our dominant thoughts, so we need to make sure our thoughts line up with what we desire. Believing that we have Christ's "raising-from-the-dead" power living inside of us makes it a lot more likely that we will see miraculous results when we pray. If we don't believe that we have authority over sickness, we are not likely to see very good results when we tell sickness to leave our bodies. As we think, that's the way we are (Prov. 23:7): If we think we are powerless, we will be.

It saddens me to see how far below their privileges many Christians live. They believe they will be healed if I or another minister prays for them, but they haven't renewed their minds to believe God will do it for them. I've seen all kinds of healings and miracles, but I don't have a special anointing for healing. I don't have anything that "Joe Blow believer" doesn't have. The only reason I might see better results than most people is because I know what God has given me—and I use it.

God Almighty lives on the inside of every believer, yet we act like He's out in space somewhere. We think the devil is blocking our prayers from getting through to God, so we do "spiritual warfare" and get a hundred million people to pray and open up the heavens so that our prayers can get through. We don't need to do that. God isn't waiting for us to try hard enough before He answers our prayers. No, God lives on the inside of us, and He says that He is never going to leave us nor forsake us (Heb. 13:5). We don't have to get our prayers past demons in order for them to reach God—or enlist enough prayer warriors to force God to listen to our prayers. Weird doctrines like that only come up because we don't know what the Word says.

Have you ever heard the expression *what you don't know won't hurt you,* or *ignorance is bliss*? Well, both of those statements are lies. What you don't know *is* killing you. You've been squeezed into the mold of the world, and your ignorance of the truths in God's Word *is* killing you. You have to renew your mind if you want to find, follow, and fulfill your God-given purpose in life. Making a commitment to the Lord is a start, but you have to get into the Word of God. You need to get to where you know God's Word better than you know what's happening on your favorite television show. I enjoy watching the old Wile E. Coyote and The Road Runner cartoons. I think they're funny. But if that's all I'm full of, then in a crisis situation, when I open my mouth, all that would come out would be "Beep! Beep!" And I'm going to be in trouble.

Whatever we focus our attention on is what will dominate our thoughts (Prov. 23:7). If our thoughts are dominated by the things of this world, then we are going to get worldly results in our lives. We need to focus on God to get godly results. That's why Jesus admonished us to *"seek ye first the kingdom of God"* (Matt. 6:33). We shouldn't be absorbed by what's going on in the world—by all of this stuff that doesn't amount to anything. We need to have an eternal focus.

People who are struggling and haven't seen God's will manifest in their lives probably haven't renewed their minds to God's way of thinking. Don't be discouraged if you suspect that you fall into that category. Now that you know what the problem is, you can fix it. Renew your mind with the Word of God, and you will prove the good, acceptable, and perfect will of God. It's that simple. Having done that, you would have to rebel against God to miss His will for your life. After you renew your mind, you can count on seeing God's will come to pass in your life. All you have to do is commit yourself to the Word of God, and you will see some awesome things begin to happen.

OUTLINE • 4.2

V. People know that God can do anything, so they ask Him to rearrange their entire lives in an instant, but not everything happens by prayer alone.

    A. Jesus taught that the kingdom of God also operates like a seed (Matt. 13:31)—the seed you have to plant to get kingdom results is the Word of God (Luke 8:11).

    B. If you want to have prayers that are regularly answered, you have to sow the Word.

    C. The Word of God shows you God's way of thinking.

        i. It renews your mind.

        ii. It tears down the obstacles that prevent you from freely receiving all that Christ has already purchased for you.

    D. A limited understanding of God's Word won't get you far.

VI. The majority of believers aren't renewing their minds—they let their minds be polluted by focusing on what's happening in the world.

    A. Whenever disaster strikes, Christians get into the same fear as unbelievers because they are poured into the mold of this world, instead of having their minds renewed by the Word of God and being poured into His image.

    B. Meditating on the Word will make us think differently than the world.

    C. We shouldn't have the same fear-based reactions as people who don't know Jesus.

        i. We are spiritually alive; they are spiritually dead—that's a big difference.

    D. We should adopt God's way of thinking.

VII. Jesus said that the Word of God is the truth (John 17:17).

    A. The truth is what sets you free—and it's only the truth you *know* that sets you free (John 8:32).

    B. You have to read the Bible and know what it says, not just say you believe it.

    C. A lot of people are worried that the Word will lose its freshness or that it will become boring like a novel if they read it all—but that will never happen.

    D. I've read through the Bible hundreds of times, and I get more out of it every time I read it.

    E. It almost seems like you have to spend thirty years in the Bible just to learn enough to ask the right questions.

F. I'm just now beginning to understand the Word in ways I never have before.

G. Even if you have read the Bible once, I guarantee that you didn't get it all.

H. You need to be studying the Word and renewing your mind with it on a daily basis.

VIII. God has given every born-again believer the same authority.

A. Once you recognize who you are in Christ, you can take your authority, speak to your body, and command sickness to leave.

B. Many Christians don't realize what God has *already* done for them, so they go to God like a beggar—pleading for an answer to prayer.

C. You need to get rid of that *stinking thinking* because it's killing you.

IX. If Jesus was here in His physical body today, He would not be pleased with our inability.

A. In the Gospel of Matthew, chapter 17, Jesus' disciples brought a man to Him because they had been unable to cast a demon out of the man's son.

B. Jesus called them a faithless and perverse group of people and said, *"How long shall I be with you? how long shall I suffer you? bring him hither to me"* (Matt. 17:17).

C. At the time of that story, the disciples didn't have the advantages we have: We have born-again spirits, we are empowered by the Holy Spirit to do the works that Jesus did, and we have the truth of God's Word at our fingertips.

D. Yet the sick people who come to us for healing aren't always being delivered to the degree that they should be.

E. Jesus told us to meet the needs of people, but we aren't even coming close.

X. Transformation comes by renewing the mind, so in order to experience positive changes in our lives, we need to change the way we think.

A. Our lives go in the direction of our dominant thoughts, so we need to make sure our thoughts line up with what we desire.

B. Believing that we have Christ's "raising-from-the-dead" power living inside of us makes it a lot more likely that we will see miraculous results when we pray.

C. If we don't believe that we have authority over sickness, we are not likely to see very good results when we tell sickness to leave our bodies.

D. As we think, that's the way we are (Prov. 23:7): If we think we are powerless, we will be.

XI. It saddens me to see how far below their privileges many Christians live.

A. The only reason I might see better results than most people is because I know what God has given me—and I use it.

B. God isn't waiting for us to try hard enough before He answers our prayers.

C. He lives on the inside of us, and He says that He is never going to leave us nor forsake us (Heb. 13:5).

D. We don't have to get our prayers past demons in order for them to reach God—or enlist enough prayer warriors to force God to listen to our prayers.

E. Weird doctrines like that only come up because we don't know what the Word says.

XII. You've been squeezed into the mold of the world, and your ignorance of the truths in God's Word *is* killing you.

A. You have to renew your mind if you want to find, follow, and fulfill your God-given purpose in life.

B. Making a commitment to the Lord is a start, but you have to get into the Word of God.

C. You need to focus on God to get godly results.

D. You shouldn't be absorbed by what's going on in the world—by all of this stuff that doesn't amount to anything.

XIII. People who are struggling and haven't seen God's will manifest in their lives probably haven't renewed their minds to God's way of thinking.

A. Don't be discouraged if you suspect that you fall into that category—now that you know what the problem is, you can fix it.

B. Renew your mind with the Word of God, and you will prove the good, acceptable, and perfect will of God—it's that simple.

C. After you renew your mind, you can count on seeing God's will come to pass in your life.

5. People know that God can do anything, so they ask Him to rearrange their entire lives in an instant, but not everything happens by prayer alone. Jesus taught that the kingdom of God also operates like a seed (Matt. 13:31)—the seed you have to plant to get kingdom results is the Word of God (Luke 8:11). If you want to have prayers that are regularly answered, you have to sow the Word. The Word of God shows you God's way of thinking. It renews your mind. It tears down the obstacles that prevent you from freely receiving all that Christ has already purchased for you. A limited understanding of God's Word won't get you far.

5a.　True or false: Not everything happens by prayer alone.
True

5b.　What is the Word of God?
God's way of thinking

5c.　A limited _____ of God's Word won't get you far.
Understanding

6. The majority of believers aren't renewing their minds—they let their minds be polluted by focusing on what's happening in the world. Whenever disaster strikes, Christians get into the same fear as unbelievers because they are poured into the mold of this world, instead of having their minds renewed by the Word of God and being poured into His image. Meditating on the Word will make us think differently than the world. We shouldn't have the same fear-based reactions as people who don't know Jesus. We are spiritually alive; they are spiritually dead—that's a big difference. We should adopt God's way of thinking.

6a.　What will make you think differently than the world?
　　A.　The best new soap opera
　　B.　The most popular minister
　　C.　Political power and influence
　　D.　Meditating on the Word
　　E.　A major university
D.　Meditating on the Word

6b.　Why shouldn't you have the same fear-based reactions as people who don't know Jesus?
You are spiritually alive; they are spiritually dead

7. Jesus said that the Word of God is the truth (John 17:17). The truth is what sets you free—and it's only the truth you *know* that sets you free (John 8:32). You have to read the Bible and know what it says, not just say you believe it. A lot of people are worried that the Word will lose its freshness or that it will become boring like a novel if they read it all—but that will never happen. I've read through the Bible hundreds of times, and I get more out of it every time I read it. It almost seems like you have to spend thirty years in the Bible just to learn enough to ask the right questions. I'm just now beginning to understand the Word in ways I never have before. Even if you have read the Bible once, I guarantee that you didn't get it all. You need to be studying the Word and renewing your mind with it on a daily basis.

7a.   Read John 17:17. Who said the Word of God is the truth?
Jesus

7b.   According to John 8:32, it's only the truth you _____ that sets you free.
Know

7c.   True or false: It's enough just to say you believe the Bible.
False

7d.   Discussion question: In what ways has the Bible not been boring to you?
Discussion question

7e.   True or false: If you have read the Bible once, it's possible that you got it all.
False

7f.   How often do you need to study the Word and renew your mind with it?
On a daily basis

8. God has given every born-again believer the same authority. Once you recognize who you are in Christ, you can take your authority, speak to your body, and command sickness to leave. Many Christians don't realize what God has *already* done for them, so they go to God like a beggar—pleading for an answer to prayer. You need to get rid of that *stinking thinking* because it's killing you.

8a.   What can you do once you recognize your authority?
    A.   You can give your authority, speak to your body, and command sickness to leave
    B.   You can take your authority, speak to your body, and ask sickness to leave
    C.   You can take your authority, speak to your body, and command sickness to leave
    D.   All of the above
    E.   None of the above
    C. You can take your authority, speak to your body, and command sickness to leave

8b.   Many Christians don't realize what God has *already* done for them, so they go to God like a _____—pleading for an answer to prayer.
Beggar

8c.   Discussion question: How can stinking thinking kill you?
Discussion question

9. If Jesus was here in His physical body today, He would not be pleased with our inability. In the Gospel of Matthew, chapter 17, Jesus' disciples brought a man to Him because they had been unable to cast a demon out of the man's son. Jesus called them a faithless and perverse group of people and said, *"How long shall I be with you? how long shall I suffer you? bring him hither to me"* (Matt. 17:17). At the time of that story, the disciples didn't have the advantages we have: We have born-again spirits, we are empowered by the Holy Spirit to do the works that Jesus did, and we have the truth of God's Word at our fingertips. Yet the sick people who come to us for healing aren't always being delivered to the degree that they should be. Jesus told us to meet the needs of people, but we aren't even coming close.

9a.   Discussion question: Why aren't the sick people who come to us for healing always being delivered to the degree that they should be?
Discussion question

10. Transformation comes by renewing the mind, so in order to experience positive changes in our lives, we need to change the way we think. Our lives go in the direction of our dominant thoughts, so we need to make sure our thoughts line up with what we desire. Believing that we have Christ's "raising-from-the-dead" power living inside of us makes it a lot more likely that we will see miraculous results when we pray. If we don't believe that we have authority over sickness, we are not likely to see very good results when we tell sickness to leave our bodies. As we think, that's the way we are (Prov. 23:7): If we think we are powerless, we will be.

10a.   In order to experience positive changes in your life, what do you need to do?
You need to change the way you think

10b.   Your life goes in the direction of what?
A.   Where you point
B.   The last thing you heard
C.   What you can afford
D.   Where most people are going
E.   Your dominant thoughts
E.   Your dominant thoughts

10c.   True or false: If you don't believe that you have authority over sickness, you are not likely to see very good results when you tell sickness to leave your body.
True

10d.   Read Proverbs 23:7. If you think you are powerless, you _____ be.
Will

11. It saddens me to see how far below their privileges many Christians live. The only reason I might see better results than most people is because I know what God has given me—and I use it. God isn't waiting for us to try hard enough before He answers our prayers. He lives on the inside of us, and He says that He is never going to leave us nor forsake us (Heb. 13:5). We don't have to get our prayers past demons in order for them to reach God—or enlist enough prayer warriors to force God to listen to our prayers. Weird doctrines like that only come up because we don't know what the Word says.

11a. If you know what God has given you, and you use it, you will see what?
Better results

11b. True or false: God is waiting for you to try hard enough before He answers your prayers.
False

11c. Discussion question: Why is it important to know that God will never leave you nor forsake you?
Discussion question

11d. Weird doctrines only come up when?
   A. You don't know what the Word says
   B. You watch the news
   C. You have too much time to yourself
   D. All of the above
   E. None of the above
   A. You don't know what the Word says

12. You've been squeezed into the mold of the world, and your ignorance of the truths in God's Word *is* killing you. You have to renew your mind if you want to find, follow, and fulfill your God-given purpose in life. Making a commitment to the Lord is a start, but you have to get into the Word of God. You need to focus on God to get godly results. You shouldn't be absorbed by what's going on in the world—by all of this stuff that doesn't amount to anything.

12a. What will your ignorance of God's Word do to you?
Kill you

12b. You shouldn't be absorbed by what's going on in the world—by all of this stuff that doesn't _____ to anything.
Amount

13. People who are struggling and haven't seen God's will manifest in their lives probably haven't renewed their minds to God's way of thinking. Don't be discouraged if you suspect that you fall into that category—now that you know what the problem is, you can fix it. Renew your mind with the Word of God, and you will prove the good, acceptable, and perfect will of God—it's that simple. After you renew your mind, you can count on seeing God's will come to pass in your life.

13a. People who are struggling and haven't seen God's will manifest in their lives probably haven't what?
Renewed their minds to God's way of thinking

13b. Why shouldn't you be discouraged if you suspect that you fall into that category?
Because now that you know what the problem is, you can fix it

13c. After you renew your mind, you can _____ on seeing God's will come to pass in your life.
Count

13. True or false: Not everything happens by prayer alone.

14. What is the Word of God?

_____

_____

_____

15. A limited _____ of God's Word won't get you far.

16. What will make you think differently than the world?
    A. The best new soap opera
    B. The most popular minister
    C. Political power and influence
    D. Meditating on the Word
    E. A major university

17. Why shouldn't you have the same fear-based reactions as people who don't know Jesus?

_____

_____

_____

18. Read John 17:17. Who said the Word of God is the truth?

_____

_____

_____

19. According to John 8:32, it's only the truth you _____ that sets you free.

20. True or false: It's enough just to say you believe the Bible.

21. Discussion question: In what ways has the Bible not been boring to you?

_____

_____

_____

22. True or false: If you have read the Bible once, it's possible that you got it all.

23. How often do you need to study the Word and renew your mind with it?

_____

_____

_____

24. What can you do once you recognize your authority?
    A. You can give your authority, speak to your body, and command sickness to leave
    B. You can take your authority, speak to your body, and ask sickness to leave
    C. You can take your authority, speak to your body, and command sickness to leave
    D. All of the above
    E. None of the above

25. Many Christians don't realize what God has *already* done for them, so they go to God like a _____—pleading for an answer to prayer.

26. Discussion question: How can stinking thinking kill you?

_____

_____

_____

27. Discussion question: Why aren't the sick people who come to us for healing always being delivered to the degree that they should be?

_____

_____

_____

28. In order to experience positive changes in your life, what do you need to do?

_____

_____

_____

29. Your life goes in the direction of what?
    A. Where you point
    B. The last thing you heard
    C. What you can afford
    D. Where most people are going
    E. Your dominant thoughts

30. True or false: If you don't believe that you have authority over sickness, you are not likely to see very good results when you tell sickness to leave your body.

31. Read Proverbs 23:7. If you think you are powerless, you _____ be.

32. If you know what God has given you, and you use it, you will see what?

_____

_____

_____

33. True or false: God is waiting for you to try hard enough before He answers your prayers.

34. Discussion question: Why is it important to know that God will never leave you nor forsake you?

_____

_____

_____

35. Weird doctrines only come up when?
    A. You don't know what the Word says
    B. You watch the news
    C. You have too much time to yourself
    D. All of the above
    E. None of the above

36. What will your ignorance of God's Word do to you?

_____

_____

_____

37. You shouldn't be absorbed by what's going on in the world—by all of this stuff that doesn't _____ to anything.

38. People who are struggling and haven't seen God's will manifest in their lives probably haven't what?

_____

_____

_____

39. Why shouldn't you be discouraged if you suspect that you fall into that category?

_____

_____

_____

40. After you renew your mind, you can _____ on seeing God's will come to pass in your life.

13. True
14. God's way of thinking
15. Understanding
16. D. Meditating on the Word
17. You are spiritually alive; they are spiritually dead
18. Jesus
19. Know
20. False
21. *Discussion question*
22. False
23. On a daily basis
24. C. You can take your authority, speak to your body, and command sickness to leave
25. Beggar
26. *Discussion question*
27. *Discussion question*
28. You need to change the way you think
29. E. Your dominant thoughts
30. True
31. Will
32. Better results
33. False
34. *Discussion question*
35. A. You don't know what the Word says
36. Kill you
37. Amount
38. Renewed their minds to God's way of thinking
39. Because now that you know what the problem is, you can fix it
40. Count

1 PETER 1:23

Being born again, not of corruptible seed, but of incorruptible, by the word of God, which liveth and abideth for ever.

MARK 4:13-14

And he said unto them, Know ye not this parable? and how then will ye know all parables? [14] The sower soweth the word.

MATTHEW 13:31

Another parable put he forth unto them, saying, The kingdom of heaven is like to a grain of mustard seed, which a man took, and sowed in his field.

LUKE 8:11

Now the parable is this: The seed is the word of God.

JOHN 14:1

Let not your heart be troubled: ye believe in God, believe also in me.

PSALM 46:1-2

God is our refuge and strength, a very present help in trouble. [2] Therefore will not we fear, though the earth be removed, and though the mountains be carried into the midst of the sea.

JOHN 8:32

And ye shall know the truth, and the truth shall make you free.

JOHN 17:17

Sanctify them through thy truth: thy word is truth.

JAMES 4:7

Submit yourselves therefore to God. Resist the devil, and he will flee from you.

MATTHEW 17:17

Then Jesus answered and said, O faithless and perverse generation, how long shall I be with you? how long shall I suffer you? bring him hither to me.

PROVERBS 23:7

For as he thinketh in his heart, so is he: Eat and drink, saith he to thee; but his heart is not with thee.

HEBREWS 13:5

Let your conversation be without covetousness; and be content with such things as ye have: for he hath said, I will never leave thee, nor forsake thee.

MATTHEW 6:33

But seek ye first the kingdom of God, and his righteousness; and all these things shall be added unto you.

YOUR SPIRITUAL
IDENTITY

LESSON 5.1

I can't overemphasize how essential the Word of God is in discovering our spiritual identity and finding God's will for our lives. A lot of people look at the Bible and think, *This book was written thousands of years ago; what does it have to do with me?* The Bible isn't just another book; it is quick—which means alive—and powerful. It reveals things to us that we could never figure out on our own.

> *For the word of God is quick, and powerful, and sharper than any twoedged sword, piercing even to the dividing asunder of soul and spirit, and of the joints and marrow, and is a discerner of the thoughts and intents of the heart.*
> HEBREWS 4:12

This scripture implies that to know the difference between soul and spirit is hard. And it is. In fact, most people don't know the difference. Functionally, most people think the soul and spirit are the same. But the spirit is the part of us that was born again when we believed in Jesus. Our spirits are identical to Jesus. We have gifts of the Holy Spirit, such as love, joy, peace, long-suffering, gentleness, goodness, faith, meekness, and temperance (Gal. 5:22-23). Those things are always in our spirits—they have been there since the moment we were born again. In our spirits, we have the mind of Christ and an unction from the Holy Spirit and know all things (1 Cor. 2:16 and 1 John 2:20).

Some people are going to read this and think, *That can't be true. I live in turmoil, I don't have any peace, and I sure don't know all things.* But it isn't our minds that know everything; you can prove that. Many of us have searched the house looking for keys that were in our pockets the whole time. We are wrong more often than we like to admit, and our natural minds obviously don't know everything there is to know. But in our spirits, we know all things. The mind is physical, and we cannot perceive spiritual things by carnal means. The mind has to do with sense knowledge (what we see, taste, hear, smell, and feel). It is a part of our souls, and the soul isn't made completely new when we are born again—our spirits are.

In our spirits, we are identical to Jesus. We have His power, anointing, wisdom, joy, peace, and love because the Holy Spirit is continually producing fruit in our spirits.

Our senses might be telling us that the world is caving in, but in our born-again spirits, we have love, joy, and peace. The only way we can know what we have in our spirits is through the Word of God—it will divide between soul and spirit. The Word will show us who we are, no matter how we feel.

Finding God's will is really as simple as discerning whether our feelings are coming from the spirit or the flesh. It's simple, but it isn't easy, because most of us don't know what is true in our spirits. We are dominated by what we can see, taste, hear, smell, and feel. We don't think spiritually.

The Apostle John wrote that as Jesus is, so are we in this world (1 John 4:17). He didn't say that you will be like Jesus after you die and go to heaven; he said *so are you in this world*. In your spirit, you are identical to Jesus. I know that can be hard to believe, but it's true. When you look in the mirror, you may see zits, gray hair, and bulges, and think, *I sure don't look like Jesus*. True, your physical body isn't like Jesus, but your *spirit* is identical to Him. As humans, people tend to assume that if their spirits are identical to Jesus, they would just know it somehow. They think, *If I had love, I'd know it*. Not true. The Bible says,

> *But the natural man receiveth not the things of the Spirit of God: for they are foolishness unto him: neither can he know them, because they are spiritually discerned.*
>
> 1 CORINTHIANS 2:14

Our little "peanut" brains don't know what happened to our spirits when we were born again. *So, our intellect doesn't know our spiritual identity*. Some things can only be discerned spiritually. We can't look in a mirror and see our spirits. We can't feel around and sense our spirits. We can't try to feel with our emotions to see if we have joy in our spirits. Our spirits can't be felt by our physical senses. But the Word of God will show us what we don't intuitively know.

Jesus told His disciples, *"The words that I speak unto you, they are spirit, and they are life"* (John 6:63). The only way we can know what's going on in the spirit is through the Word. The Word shows us our spiritual identity. If we don't know the Word of God, we won't know who we are in our spirits. Our physical senses will dominate us, even though the whole time, we have living inside of us the same Spirit that raised Christ from the dead (Rom. 8:9 with Eph. 1:19-20). The only way we are going to get what is in our spirits to flow out into our lives is by letting the Word of God speak to us and direct us.

It took me twenty years to understand everything I've just told you. This is powerful stuff. I guarantee you that understanding the makeup of the spirit, soul, and body will transform your life.[1] But most people let this go right over their heads. They don't let the Word of God reveal to them who they are and what they have. People are begging God for results, instead of taking the Word of God and finding out their identity in Christ and using the Word like a sword.

You've Already Got It

> *Simon Peter, a servant and an apostle of Jesus Christ, to them that have obtained like precious faith with us through the righteousness of God and our Saviour Jesus Christ.*
>
> 2 PETER 1:1

The Apostle Peter wrote this letter to people who have "*like precious faith.*" If you look that up in the Greek, it means identical faith. This was written to people who have the identical faith that Peter had. If you say "Oh, I could never claim that," then just go ahead and tear 2 Peter out of your Bible, because that's who Peter was writing to. Everyone who has been born again has as much faith as Peter had. Peter walked on water (Matt. 14:29). He saw Dorcas raised from the dead (Acts 9:39-40). His shadow healed people as it passed over them (Acts 5:15). Peter did great miracles. And you have the same faith he had!

Every person who has been born again and baptized in the Holy Spirit has enough power and anointing on the inside of them to raise the dead, walk on water, and have their shadow heal people. Every single believer has this power. Somebody might say, "Yeah, I have faith, but it's just in little seed form. It hasn't grown yet." That's not true; your faith isn't growing. Faith is complete. You already have the fullness of faith on the inside. The problem is that you don't know what you have. You just need to renew your mind.

> *That the communication of thy faith may become effectual by the acknowledging of every good thing which is in you in Christ Jesus.*
>
> PHILEMON 6

The way your faith becomes effectual, or the way it begins to work, is by *acknowledging what you already have*. You don't need God to give you more faith. Every believer is given the same measure of faith at salvation (Rom. 12:3, 2 Pet. 1:1, and Gal. 2:20). You need to use what God has already given you. Once, the disciples asked Jesus to increase their faith, and He told them to use what they had (Luke 17:5-10). You don't need more faith; you need to realize that *you already have faith*. The Word of God shows you what you have. After introducing his letter by saying that he was writing it to those who have "*like precious faith,*" Peter wrote,

Grace and peace be multiplied unto you through the knowledge of God, and of Jesus our Lord, [3] According as his divine power hath given unto us all things that pertain unto life and godliness, through the knowledge of him that hath called us to glory and virtue: [4] Whereby are given unto us exceeding great and precious promises: that by these ye might be partakers of the divine nature, having escaped the corruption that is in the world through lust.

2 PETER 1:2-4

Grace and peace are multiplied through the knowledge of God and Jesus Christ. If you don't have knowledge, you aren't going to have peace. It doesn't matter how much you pray—you can have people pray for you until they rub all the hair off the top of your head—but you still won't have God's peace until you renew your mind. You can't operate contrary to your dominant thoughts. If you are focused on the problems you have and all that is going wrong in the world, you won't have peace. God keeps you in perfect peace when you keep your mind focused on Jesus (Is. 26:3).

Notice that the Scripture says God *has* given us *all things* according to the knowledge of Him. We receive all the fullness of God through salvation. We experience this fullness by renewing our minds with the Word of God. In a sense, any problems we have in life are knowledge problems. Peace, healing, and direction all come through the knowledge of God that is revealed in His Word. We just need to know who we are and what we have in our spirits.

Jesus said that He came to give us life and to give it abundantly (John 10:10). He came to give us a life that is full of blessings. He proved this by going around healing everyone who was oppressed by the devil (Acts 10:38). Everything that it takes to have an abundant life comes through knowing God: healing, joy, peace, prosperity, abundance, vision, and every blessing.

The Word of God is the knowledge of God, and everything we need comes through it. But the promise of everything coming through the knowledge of God assumes that we are going to act on the knowledge we have. Faith without works is dead (James 2:20). Prosperity, for instance, comes when we know what the Word says and act on that knowledge. Likewise, we have health in our bodies when we know that Jesus provided healing on the cross and take the steps to receive what the Lord has already provided. But if we don't act on what we know, we can miss out on the prosperity and healing God desires us to possess.

No problem exists that is bigger than God's supply. Whatever problem we might have, God can handle it. We just need to get away from being pressed into thinking the way the world thinks and renew our minds to the truth that *nothing is impossible for God*! We have to stop believing who the world says we are and find out who God says we are. We will find our spiritual identity in God's Word.

Andrew's Recommendations for Further Study:

[1]I encourage you to get my teaching *Spirit, Soul & Body*. It goes into a lot more detail on this than I'm able to cover here and is foundational to understanding this.

OUTLINE • 5.1

I.   I can't overemphasize how essential the Word of God is in discovering our spiritual identity and finding God's will for our lives.

   A.   The Bible reveals things to us that we could never figure out on our own.

     For the word of God is quick, and powerful, and sharper than any twoedged sword, piercing even to the dividing asunder of soul and spirit, and of the joints and marrow, and is a discerner of the thoughts and intents of the heart.
                      HEBREWS 4:12

   B.   Functionally, most people think the soul and spirit are the same, but the spirit is the part of us that was born again when we believed in Jesus.

      i.   Our spirits are identical to Jesus.

      ii.   We have gifts of the Holy Spirit, such as love, joy, peace, long-suffering, gentleness, goodness, faith, meekness, and temperance (Gal. 5:22-23) in our spirits.

      iii.   We also have the mind of Christ and an unction from the Holy Spirit and know all things (1 Cor. 2:16 and 1 John 2:20).

   C.   The soul isn't made completely new when we are born again—our spirits are.

   D.   The only way we can know what we have in our spirits is through the Word of God—it will divide between soul and spirit.

   E.   Finding God's will is really as simple as discerning whether our feelings are coming from the spirit or the flesh.

   F.   It's simple, but it isn't easy, because most of us don't know what is true in our spirits.

II.   The Apostle John wrote that as Jesus is, so are we in this world (1 John 4:17).

   A.   Our physical bodies aren't like Jesus, but our *spirits* are identical to Him.

   B.   As humans, we tend to assume that if our spirits are identical to Jesus, we would just know it somehow, but that's not true.

     But the natural man receiveth not the things of the Spirit of God: for they are foolishness unto him: neither can he know them, because they are spiritually discerned.
                  1 CORINTHIANS 2:14

   C.   Our little "peanut" brains don't know what happened to our spirits when we were born again, *so our intellect doesn't know our spiritual identity.*

   D.   Some things can only be discerned spiritually.

III. Jesus told His disciples, *"The words that I speak unto you, they are spirit, and they are life"* (John 6:63).

    A. If we don't know the Word of God, we won't know who we are in our spirits.

    B. Our physical senses will dominate us, even though the whole time we have living inside of us the same Spirit that raised Christ from the dead (Rom. 8:9 with Eph. 1:19-20).

    C. The only way we are going to get what is in our spirits to flow out into our lives is by letting the Word of God speak to us and direct us.

    D. Understanding the makeup of the spirit, soul, and body will transform our lives[1], because many of us are begging God for results instead of taking the Word of God and finding out our identity in Christ and using the Word like a sword.

IV. In 2 Peter 1:1, *"like precious faith"* in the Greek means identical faith.

    A. Everyone who has been born again has as much faith as Peter had.

        i. Peter walked on water (Matt. 14:29).

        ii. He saw Dorcas raised from the dead (Acts 9:39-40).

        iii. His shadow healed people as it passed over them (Acts 5:15).

    B. Somebody might say "Yeah, I have faith, but it's just in little seed form. It hasn't grown yet," but your faith isn't growing—you already have the fullness of faith on the inside.

    C. The way your faith becomes effectual, or the way it begins to work, is by *acknowledging what you already have* (Philem. 6).

    D. You don't need more faith; you need to realize that *you already have faith.*

V. *Grace and peace are multiplied through the knowledge of God and Jesus Christ* (2 Pet. 1:2-4).

    A. It doesn't matter how much you pray—you can have people pray for you until they rub all the hair off the top of your head—but you still won't have God's peace until you renew your mind.

    B. You can't operate contrary to your dominant thoughts.

    C. God keeps you in perfect peace when you keep your mind focused on Jesus (Is. 26:3).

VI. Notice that the Scripture says God *has* given us *all things* according to the knowledge of Him (2 Pet. 1:3).

    A. We receive all the fullness of God through salvation and experience it by renewing our minds with the Word of God.

B. In a sense, any problems we have in life are knowledge problems.

C. Jesus said that He came to give us life and to give it abundantly (John 10:10)—and everything that it takes to have an abundant life comes through knowing God: healing, joy, peace, prosperity, abundance, vision, and every blessing.

D. But the promise of everything coming through the knowledge of God assumes that we are going to act on the knowledge we have.

    i. Prosperity, for instance, comes when we know what the Word says and act on that knowledge.

    ii. Likewise, we have health in our bodies when we know that Jesus provided healing on the cross and take the steps to receive what the Lord has already provided.

VII. No problem exists that is bigger than God's supply.

A. We just need to get away from being pressed into thinking the way the world thinks and renew our minds to the truth that *nothing is impossible for God*!

B. We have to stop believing who the world says we are and find out who God says we are.

C. We will find our spiritual identity in God's Word.

Andrew's Recommendations for Further Study:

[1]I encourage you to get my teaching *Spirit, Soul & Body*. It goes into a lot more detail on this than I'm able to cover here and is foundational to understanding this.

1. I can't overemphasize how essential the Word of God is in discovering our spiritual identity and finding God's will for our lives. The Bible reveals things to us that we could never figure out on our own.

> *For the word of God is quick, and powerful, and sharper than any twoedged sword, piercing even to the dividing asunder of soul and spirit, and of the joints and marrow, and is a discerner of the thoughts and intents of the heart.*
>
> HEBREWS 4:12

Functionally, most people think the soul and spirit are the same, but the spirit is the part of us that was born again when we believed in Jesus. Our spirits are identical to Jesus. We have gifts of the Holy Spirit, such as love, joy, peace, long-suffering, gentleness, goodness, faith, meekness, and temperance (Gal. 5:22-23) in our spirits. We also have the mind of Christ and an unction from the Holy Spirit and know all things (1 Cor. 2:16 and 1 John 2:20). The soul isn't made completely new when we are born again—our spirits are. The only way we can know what we have in our spirits is through the Word of God—it will divide between soul and spirit. Finding God's will is really as simple as discerning whether our feelings are coming from the spirit or the flesh. It's simple, but it isn't easy, because most of us don't know what is true in our spirits.

1a.   True or false: Without the Bible, you could still figure things out on your own.
      False

1b.   What is the part of you that was born again when you believed in Jesus?
      A. Your spirit
      B. Your soul
      C. Your body
      D. All of the above
      E. None of the above
      A. Your spirit

1c.   Your spirit is identical to _____.
      Jesus

1d.   True or false: The soul isn't made completely new when you are born again.
      True

1e.   Why is the Word of God the only way you can know what you have in your spirit?
      Because the Word of God divides between soul and spirit

1f.   Discussion question: How do you know that finding God's will is really as simple as discerning whether our feelings are coming from the spirit or the flesh?
      Discussion question

2. The Apostle John wrote that as Jesus is, so are we in this world (1 John 4:17). Our physical bodies aren't like Jesus, but our *spirits* are identical to Him. As humans, we tend to assume that if our spirits are identical to Jesus, we would just know it somehow, but that's not true.

> *But the natural man receiveth not the things of the Spirit of God: for they are foolishness unto him: neither can he know them, because they are spiritually discerned.*
>
> 1 CORINTHIANS 2:14

Our little "peanut" brains don't know what happened to our spirits when we were born again, *so our intellect doesn't know our spiritual identity.* Some things can only be discerned spiritually.

2a.   Read 1 John 4:17. As Jesus _____, so are you in this world.
        Is

2b.   True or false: Your body is like Jesus'.
        False

2c.   What is a human assumption?
        That if your spirit is identical to Jesus, you would just know it somehow

2d.   Read 1 Corinthians 2:14. Some things can only be discerned how?
        A. Mathematically
        B. Spiritually
        C. Carnally
        D. All of the above
        E. None of the above
        B. Spiritually

3. Jesus told His disciples, *"The words that I speak unto you, they are spirit, and they are life"* (John 6:63). If we don't know the Word of God, we won't know who we are in our spirits. Our physical senses will dominate us, even though the whole time we have living inside of us the same Spirit that raised Christ from the dead (Rom. 8:9 with Eph. 1:19-20). The only way we are going to get what is in our spirits to flow out into our lives is by letting the Word of God speak to us and direct us. Understanding the makeup of the spirit, soul, and body will transform our lives[1], because many of us are begging God for results instead of taking the Word of God and finding out our identity in Christ and using the Word like a sword.

3a.   Read John 6:63. If you don't know the Word of God, you won't know what?
        Who you are in your spirit

3b.   Read Romans 8:9 with Ephesians 1:19-20. What else will happen if you don't know the Word of God?
        Your physical senses will dominate you, even though the whole time you have living inside of you the same Spirit that raised Christ from the dead

3c.   Discussion question: What are some things the Word of God has shown you about who you are?
        Discussion question

4. In 2 Peter 1:1, *"like precious faith"* in the Greek means identical faith. Everyone who has been born again has as much faith as Peter had. Peter walked on water (Matt. 14:29). He saw Dorcas raised from the dead (Acts 9:39-40). His shadow healed people as it passed over them (Acts 5:15). Somebody might say "Yeah, I have faith, but it's just in little seed form. It hasn't grown yet," but your faith isn't growing—you already have the fullness of faith on the inside. The way your faith becomes effectual, or the way it begins to work, is by *acknowledging what you already have* (Philem. 6). You don't need more faith; you need to realize that *you already have faith.*

4a.   Read 2 Peter 1:1. What does *"like precious faith"* mean?
        Identical faith

4b.   Are there miracles Peter did that you can't do?
        No

4c.   According to Philemon 6, the way to make your faith effectual is by _____ what you already have.
        Acknowledging

5. *Grace and peace are multiplied through the knowledge of God and Jesus Christ* (2 Pet. 1:2-4). It doesn't matter how much you pray—you can have people pray for you until they rub all the hair off the top of your head—but you still won't have God's peace until you renew your mind. You can't operate contrary to your dominant thoughts. God keeps you in perfect peace when you keep your mind focused on Jesus (Is. 26:3).

5a. Read 2 Peter 1:2-4. Why won't you have peace until you renew your mind?
   A. Because peace is added through the knowledge of God and Jesus Christ
   B. Because peace is earned through the knowledge of God and Jesus Christ
   C. Because peace is multiplied through the knowledge of God and Jesus Christ
   D. Because peace is lost through the knowledge of God and Jesus Christ
   E. Because peace is divided through the knowledge of God and Jesus Christ
   C. Because peace is multiplied through the knowledge of God and Jesus Christ

5b. Discussion question: Why do you think you can't operate contrary to your dominant thoughts?
   Discussion question

6. Notice that the Scripture says God *has* given us *all things* according to the knowledge of Him (2 Pet. 1:3). We receive all the fullness of God through salvation and experience it by renewing our minds with the Word of God. In a sense, any problems we have in life are knowledge problems. Jesus said that He came to give us life and to give it abundantly (John 10:10)—and everything that it takes to have an abundant life comes through knowing God: healing, joy, peace, prosperity, abundance, vision, and every blessing. But the promise of everything coming through the knowledge of God assumes that we are going to act on the knowledge we have. Prosperity, for instance, comes when we know what the Word says and act on that knowledge. Likewise, we have health in our bodies when we know that Jesus provided healing on the cross and take the steps to receive what the Lord has already provided.

6a. True or false: You receive part of the fullness of God through salvation and experience it by renewing your mind with the Word of God.
   False

6b. The promise of everything coming through the knowledge of God assumes what?
   A. That you are going to act on the knowledge you have
   B. That you know more than what you currently do
   C. That knowledge of the Word is easy to attain
   D. All of the above
   E. None of the above
   A. That you are going to act on the knowledge you have

7. No problem exists that is bigger than God's supply. We just need to get away from being pressed into thinking the way the world thinks and renew our minds to the truth that *nothing is impossible for God*! We have to stop believing who the world says we are and find out who God says we are. We will find our spiritual identity in God's Word.

7a. Discussion question: Why is it important to renew your mind to the truth that nothing is impossible for God?
Discussion question

7b. What do you need to stop believing?
Who the world says you are

DISCIPLESHIP QUESTIONS • 5.1

1. True or false: Without the Bible, you could still figure things out on your own.

2. What is the part of you that was born again when you believed in Jesus?
    A. Your spirit
    B. Your soul
    C. Your body
    D. All of the above
    E. None of the above

3. Your spirit is identical to _____.

4. True or false: The soul isn't made completely new when you are born again.

5. Why is the Word of God the only way you can know what you have in your spirit?

    _____

    _____

    _____

6. Discussion question: How do you know that finding God's will is really as simple as discerning whether our feelings are coming from the spirit or the flesh?

    _____

    _____

    _____

7. Read 1 John 4:17. As Jesus _____, so are you in this world.

8. True or false: Your body is like Jesus'.

9. What is a human assumption?

    _____

    _____

    _____

10. Read 1 Corinthians 2:14. Some things can only be discerned how?
    A. Mathematically
    B. Spiritually
    C. Carnally
    D. All of the above
    E. None of the above

11. Read John 6:63. If you don't know the Word of God, you won't know what?

_____

_____

_____

12. Read Romans 8:9 with Ephesians 1:19-20. What else will happen if you don't know the Word of God?

_____

_____

_____

13. Discussion question: What are some things the Word of God has shown you about who you are?

_____

_____

_____

14. Read 2 Peter 1:1. What does *"like precious faith"* mean?

_____

_____

_____

15. Are there miracles Peter did that you can't do?

_____

_____

_____

16. According to Philemon 6, the way to make your faith effectual is by _____ what you already have.

17. Read 2 Peter 1:2-4. Why won't you have peace until you renew your mind?
    A. Because peace is added through the knowledge of God and Jesus Christ
    B. Because peace is earned through the knowledge of God and Jesus Christ
    C. Because peace is multiplied through the knowledge of God and Jesus Christ
    D. Because peace is lost through the knowledge of God and Jesus Christ
    E. Because peace is divided through the knowledge of God and Jesus Christ

18. Discussion question: Why do you think you can't operate contrary to your dominant thoughts?

    _____

    _____

    _____

19. True or false: You receive part of the fullness of God through salvation and experience it by renewing your mind with the Word of God.

20. The promise of everything coming through the knowledge of God assumes what?
    A. That you are going to act on the knowledge you have
    B. That you know more than what you currently do
    C. That knowledge of the Word is easy to attain
    D. All of the above
    E. None of the above

21. Discussion question: Why is it important to renew your mind to the truth that nothing is impossible for God?

    _____

    _____

    _____

22. What do you need to stop believing?

_____

_____

_____

ANSWER KEY • 5.1

1. False
2. A. Your spirit
3. Jesus
4. True
5. Because the Word of God divides between soul and spirit
6. *Discussion question*
7. Is
8. False
9. That if your spirit is identical to Jesus, you would just know it somehow
10. B. Spiritually
11. Who you are in your spirit
12. Your physical senses will dominate you, even though the whole time you have living inside of you the same Spirit that raised Christ from the dead
13. *Discussion question*
14. Identical faith
15. No
16. Acknowledging
17. C. Because peace is multiplied through the knowledge of God and Jesus Christ
18. *Discussion question*
19. False
20. A. That you are going to act on the knowledge you have
21. *Discussion question*
22. Who the world says you are

HEBREWS 4:12

For the word of God is quick, and powerful, and sharper than any twoedged sword, piercing even to the dividing asunder of soul and spirit, and of the joints and marrow, and is a discerner of the thoughts and intents of the heart.

GALATIANS 5:22-23

But the fruit of the Spirit is love, joy, peace, longsuffering, gentleness, goodness, faith, [23] Meekness, temperance: against such there is no law.

1 CORINTHIANS 2:16

For who hath known the mind of the Lord, that he may instruct him? But we have the mind of Christ.

1 JOHN 2:20

But ye have an unction from the Holy One, and ye know all things.

1 JOHN 4:17

Herein is our love made perfect, that we may have boldness in the day of judgment: because as he is, so are we in this world.

1 CORINTHIANS 2:14

But the natural man receiveth not the things of the Spirit of God: for they are foolishness unto him: neither can he know them, because they are spiritually discerned.

JOHN 6:63

It is the spirit that quickeneth; the flesh profiteth nothing: the words that I speak unto you, they are spirit, and they are life.

ROMANS 8:9

But ye are not in the flesh, but in the Spirit, if so be that the Spirit of God dwell in you. Now if any man have not the Spirit of Christ, he is none of his.

EPHESIANS 1:19-20

And what is the exceeding greatness of his power to us-ward who believe, according to the working of his mighty power, [20] Which he wrought in Christ, when he raised him from the dead, and set him at his own right hand in the heavenly places.

2 PETER 1:1-4

Simon Peter, a servant and an apostle of Jesus Christ, to them that have obtained like precious faith with us through the righteousness of God and our Saviour Jesus Christ: [2] Grace and peace be multiplied unto you through the knowledge of God, and of Jesus our Lord, [3] According as his divine power hath given unto us all things that pertain unto life and godliness, through the knowledge of him that hath called us to glory and virtue: [4] Whereby are given unto us exceeding great and precious promises: that by these ye might be partakers of the divine nature, having escaped the corruption that is in the world through lust.

MATTHEW 14:29

And he said, Come. And when Peter was come down out of the ship, he walked on the water, to go to Jesus.

ACTS 9:39-40

Then Peter arose and went with them. When he was come, they brought him into the upper chamber: and all the widows stood by him weeping, and shewing the coats and garments which Dorcas made, while she was with them. [40] But Peter put them all forth, and kneeled down, and prayed; and turning him to the body said, Tabitha, arise. And she opened her eyes: and when she saw Peter, she sat up.

ACTS 5:15

Insomuch that they brought forth the sick into the streets, and laid them on beds and couches, that at the least the shadow of Peter passing by might overshadow some of them.

PHILEMON 6

That the communication of thy faith may become effectual by the acknowledging of every good thing which is in you in Christ Jesus.

ROMANS 12:3

For I say, through the grace given unto me, to every man that is among you, not to think of himself more highly than he ought to think; but to think soberly, according as God hath dealt to every man the measure of faith.

GALATIANS 2:20

I am crucified with Christ: nevertheless I live; yet not I, but Christ liveth in me: and the life which I now live in the flesh I live by the faith of the Son of God, who loved me, and gave himself for me.

LUKE 17:5-10
And the apostles said unto the Lord, Increase our faith. [6] And the Lord said, If ye had faith as a grain of mustard seed, ye might say unto this sycamine tree, Be thou plucked up by the root, and be thou planted in the sea; and it should obey you. [7] But which of you, having a servant plowing or feeding cattle, will say unto him by and by, when he is come from the field, Go and sit down to meat? [8] And will not rather say unto him, Make ready wherewith I may sup, and gird thyself, and serve me, till I have eaten and drunken; and afterward thou shalt eat and drink? [9] Doth he thank that servant because he did the things that were commanded him? I trow not. [10] So likewise ye, when ye shall have done all those things which are commanded you, say, We are unprofitable servants: we have done that which was our duty to do.

ISAIAH 26:3
Thou wilt keep him in perfect peace, whose mind is stayed on thee: because he trusteth in thee.

JOHN 10:10
The thief cometh not, but for to steal, and to kill, and to destroy: I am come that they might have life, and that they might have it more abundantly.

ACTS 10:38
How God anointed Jesus of Nazareth with the Holy Ghost and with power: who went about doing good, and healing all that were oppressed of the devil; for God was with him.

JAMES 2:20
But wilt thou know, O vain man, that faith without works is dead?

LESSON 5.2

The longest chapter in the Bible is Psalm 119, and every verse is about the importance of the Word of God. A lot of different phrases are used to describe the Word—like the law of the Lord or the statutes of the Lord—but they all refer to the Word of God.

Wherewithal shall a young man cleanse his way? by taking heed thereto according to thy word.

PSALM 119:9

When the Lord first touched my life back in 1968, I knew that Christians were supposed to walk in power and victory. I knew there was a million times more to the Christian life than I had ever seen or heard, but I didn't know how to get from where I was to where I thought I should be. One night as I was kneeling at my bed, praying, I opened my eyes and saw my Bible lying on my bed and heard the Lord say to me, "If you put My Word in your heart, it will teach you everything you need to know." My problem was immediately solved. I began to pour myself into the Bible and renew my mind by studying the Word.

I have more understanding than all my teachers: for thy testimonies are my meditation.

PSALM 119:99

The Word of God will give us understanding. If we meditate on the Word day and night, it will make our way prosperous—then we will have good success (Josh. 1:8). We all want to be prosperous and have good success, but we want to do it without meditating in the Word day and night, because it might interfere with our television schedule or our hobbies. Although we as Christians tend to value a lot of unimportant things above the Word, God still loves us. He isn't mad at us. We can go to heaven without knowing the Word of God well. Actually, we can get to heaven quicker that way because we won't be able to receive our healing. We will die prematurely. But if we want to live victorious lives and if we want understanding, we have to meditate on the Word.

Thy word is a lamp unto my feet, and a light unto my path.

PSALM 119:105

God directs our steps, but He doesn't show us the end of the path from the very beginning. He gives us just enough light to know where to go next—He doesn't show us steps one through one hundred all at once. If He showed us everything all at once, it might overwhelm us, or we might try to rush ahead of God and take a shortcut to the end. He only shows us one step at a time because He loves us.

I have people come to me all the time who know that God wants them to attend Charis Bible College, but they hesitate because they can't see how everything is going to work out. They are trying to see the end from the beginning. I remember one guy coming into my office who said he was certain that God had told him to go to Charis, but then he started telling me all the reasons he thought it wouldn't work out. He told me about his job, his girlfriend, and the opinions of his parents and pastor. When he was finished, he said, "So, what do you think?" I said, "You lost me the moment you said God told you to do it. If God told you to do it, then forget all the rest." It's really pretty simple: If God tells you to do something—do it!

When God Almighty, who has a universe to run, takes the time to talk to you and tell you to do something, why would you try to reason it all out in order to decide whether you're going to do it or not? Something is seriously wrong with that approach. If that's the way you think, you aren't absolutely convinced that God is working for your best interest. God's plans for you are better than your plans for yourself. When the Lord tells you to do something, just do it!

I would rather step out in what I think God is telling me to do and be wrong than not do what He is telling me to because I want to play it safe. Then what would I say when I finally stood before God—"Lord, didn't You see all of the potential problems with Your plan?" God knows what He is doing and the challenges we will face. I don't want any of the miracles that God has put on the inside of me still there when I leave this world. I want to get them all out. I want to go for it!

Waiting for God to show us the whole picture before we step out is a bad plan; it isn't going to happen. God shows us His will in steps and stages. If we are out in pitch-black darkness, a lamp isn't going to illuminate something a hundred yards down the road. But it will show us the next step. That is exactly the way the Word works. As we read God's Word, He will tell us something and then we act on it. After we step into what God has said, we will be able to see the next step, and the next step, and so on.

Seed, Time, and Harvest

And he said, So is the kingdom of God, as if a man should cast seed into the ground; [27] And should sleep, and rise night and day, and the seed should spring and grow up, he knoweth not how. [28] For the earth bringeth forth fruit of herself; first the blade, then the ear, after that the full corn in the ear. [29] But when the fruit is brought forth, immediately he putteth in the sickle, because the harvest is come.

MARK 4:26-29

Seeds need time to grow. They don't immediately sprout into fruit-bearing plants. It's a process: first the blade, then the ear of corn buds, and later the full fruit of corn appears. The will of God comes in the same way: step by step. Understanding this principle will really help you.

I had a man come to me one time and show me his plans for a youth ministry project in our town. He saw a need for the youth, so his plan was to buy an abandoned Kmart building for $2 million, put another $2 million into it, and start a youth center. He showed me all of the statistics, and he was right, we did need a youth center.

So, I asked him, "Have you ever taught a Bible study?"
"No."
"Have you ever worked in a youth group?"
"No."
"Have you ever dealt with youth?"
"No."
He had never done any ministry work. I said, "It's a great idea, but it won't work for you."
"Why not?" he asked. Then he tried to justify his plans by the need.
I said, "It's first the blade, then the ear, and then the full corn in the ear. You have never been used a little bit, so you aren't going to be used a lot."

God's will for your life doesn't come to pass immediately. For you to go from zero to a thousand miles an hour instantly isn't acceleration; it's a *wreck*. It takes time to build up speed. In the same way, there is a growth process involved in finding, following, and fulfilling God's will for your life. After you have been following God's leading for a while, maybe you will begin to see a bigger picture—but you won't get it all at once.

Do One Thing

Brethren, I count not myself to have apprehended: but this one thing I do, forgetting those things which are behind, and reaching forth unto those things which are before, [14] I press toward the mark for the prize of the high calling of God in Christ Jesus.

PHILIPPIANS 3:13-14

The strength of a person lies in his or her focus. Like a laser, focus loses its power when it's diffused. If you want a laser to cut through metal, it has to be focused into a pinpoint. Paul said "*this* one *thing I do*" (emphasis mine), and that's the reason he turned the world "right-side up." You have to be focused if you want to really accomplish something.

The way to kill a person's vision is to give them two visions. Those who allow their attention to be spread around are as useless as a diffused laser. They will be distracted with the things of this world, and their understanding will be darkened. Walking in the ways of the world hinders spiritual understanding; therefore, our society is not conducive to knowing God. An ungodly, anti-Christian society promotes values and a way of life contrary to what God desires for us.

Sadly, a lot of Christians are plugged into the world, and their hearts are divided, their understanding is darkened, and they are alienated from the life of God. Many believers are ignorant of the truth of God's Word because they spend five hours a day watching junk on telvision. They read a little devotional for five minutes and think they have spent sufficient time in the Word. *Trying to build a relationship with God on scraps of discarded time is not going to bring you to the center of His will.* You have to make fellowship with God and reading His Word a priority.

The law of the LORD is perfect, converting the soul: the testimony of the LORD is sure, making wise the simple. [8] The statutes of the LORD are right, rejoicing the heart: the commandment of the LORD is pure, enlightening the eyes.

PSALM 19:7-8

The Word of God is perfect and shows you the way back to God when you lose your way. If you have made some mistakes or have been discouraged or hurt, the Word of God will convert your soul. It will restore your joy and your faith. The soul is the mental and emotional part of you that can experience turmoil—but your born-again spirit is perfect, and the Word will remind you of your true identity.

God's Word will make you wise; it will enlighten your eyes. This passage isn't talking about your physical eyes; it's talking about the ability to see with your heart: to see by faith and perceive spiritual things that your physical eyes can't see. The Word of God will open your heart to know things that you can't know by your five senses.

The Word is God is the answer for *any* and *every* problem you might have. The Bible doesn't contain man's wisdom; it contains God's wisdom for man. It's a book *from* God that contains everything you need for life and godliness. I believe the *King James* translation is the best version available, but if you can't handle the "thees" and "thous," then get a translation you enjoy reading. Getting into the Word and learning God's way of thinking is the path to finding His will for your life.

Finding God's will for your life will give you a clear purpose and keep you from getting sidetracked by the challenges you face. It's much easier to persevere through hard times when you know you are going in the right direction. Knowing that you are doing what God created you to do will give you strength to weather the storms of life.

God has never made a piece of junk. He has never made a failure. Every person born into this world was created by God for a special purpose. Everyone has the potential of becoming something beautiful. Being in the center of God's will brings a sense of fulfillment. The relationship you form with God will spill over into your life and bless the people around you. The best part is that God's will isn't hard to find—He wants you to know it! But you have to go through the narrow gate of making yourself a living sacrifice. Once you make the commitment to find God's will, you will see Him begin to move in your life, and awesome things will start to happen.

VIII. The longest chapter in the Bible is Psalm 119, and every verse is about the importance of the Word of God.

> *Wherewithal shall a young man cleanse his way? by taking heed thereto according to thy word.*
>
> PSALM 119:9

A. I knew there was a million times more to the Christian life than I had ever seen or heard, but I didn't know how to get from where I was to where I thought I should be.

B. One night, I heard the Lord say to me, "If you put My Word in your heart, it will teach you everything you need to know."

C. I began to pour myself into the Bible and renew my mind by studying the Word.

> *I have more understanding than all my teachers: for thy testimonies are my meditation.*
>
> PSALM 119:99

D. The Word of God will give us understanding.

E. If we meditate on the Word day and night, it will make our way prosperous—then we will have good success (Josh. 1:8).

F. Although we as Christians tend to value a lot of unimportant things above the Word, God still loves us.

G. But if we want to live victorious lives and if we want understanding, we have to meditate on the Word.

IX. God directs your steps, but He doesn't show you the end of the path from the very beginning (Ps. 119:105), because He loves you.

A. When God Almighty takes the time to talk to you and tell you to do something, why would you try to reason it all out in order to decide whether you're going to do it or not?

B. If that's the way you think, you aren't absolutely convinced that God is working for your best interest.

C. I would rather step out in what I think God is telling me to do and be wrong than not do what He is telling me to because I want to play it safe.

D. God knows what He is doing and the challenges you will face.

E. I don't want any of the miracles that God has put on the inside of me still there when I leave this world; I want to get them all out—I want to go for it!

F.   As you read God's Word, He will tell you something and then you act on it.

G.   After you step into what God has said, you will be able to see the next step, and the next step, and so on.

X.   Seeds don't immediately sprout into fruit-bearing plants (Mark 4:26-29).

A.   It's a process: first the blade, then the ear of corn buds, and later the full fruit of corn appears.

B.   The will of God comes in the same way: step by step.

C.   Understanding this principle will really help you.

D.   There is a growth process involved in finding, following, and fulfilling God's will for your life.

E.   After you have been following God's leading for a while, maybe you will begin to see a bigger picture—but you won't get it all at once.

XI.   The strength of a person lies in his or her focus (Phil. 3:13-14).

A.   Paul said "*this* one *thing I do*" (emphasis mine), and that's the reason he turned the world "right-side up."

B.   You have to be focused if you want to really accomplish something.

C.   The way to kill a person's vision is to give them two visions.

D.   Walking in the ways of the world hinders spiritual understanding; therefore, society is not conducive to knowing God.

E.   Sadly, a lot of Christians are plugged into the world, and their hearts are divided, their understanding is darkened, and they are alienated from the life of God.

F.   *Trying to build a relationship with God on scraps of discarded time is not going to bring you to the center of His will.*

G.   You have to make fellowship with God and reading His Word a priority.

XII.   If you have made some mistakes or have been discouraged or hurt, the Word of God will convert your soul (Ps. 19:7-8)—it will restore your joy and your faith.

A.   The soul is the mental and emotional part of you that can experience turmoil—but your born-again spirit is perfect, and the Word will remind you of your true identity.

B.   God's Word will make you wise—it will enlighten your eyes.

C.   This passage isn't talking about your physical eyes; it's talking about the ability to see with your heart: to see by faith and perceive spiritual things that your physical eyes can't see.

D. The Word of God will open your heart to know things that you can't know by your five senses.

XIII. The Word is God is the answer for *any* and *every* problem you might have.

A. The Bible contains God's wisdom for man and everything you need for life and godliness.

B. I believe that the *King James* translation is the best version available, but if you can't handle the "thees" and "thous," then get a translation you enjoy reading.

C. Getting into the Word and learning God's way of thinking is the path to finding His will for your life.

D. Finding God's will for your life will give you a clear purpose and keep you from getting sidetracked by the challenges you face.

E. Knowing that you are doing what God created you to do will give you strength to weather the storms of life.

XIV. God has never made a piece of junk—He has never made a failure.

A. Every person born into this world was created by God for a special purpose.

B. Being in the center of God's will brings a sense of fulfillment.

C. The relationship you form with God will spill over into your life and bless the people around you.

D. The best part is that God's will isn't hard to find—He wants you to know it!

E. Once you make the commitment to find God's will, you will see Him begin to move in your life, and awesome things will start to happen.

8. The longest chapter in the Bible is Psalm 119, and every verse is about the importance of the Word of God.

> *Wherewithal shall a young man cleanse his way? by taking heed thereto according to thy word.*
>
> PSALM 119:9

I knew there was a million times more to the Christian life than I had ever seen or heard, but I didn't know how to get from where I was to where I thought I should be. One night, I heard the Lord say to me, "If you put My Word in your heart, it will teach you everything you need to know." I began to pour myself into the Bible and renew my mind by studying the Word.

> *I have more understanding than all my teachers: for thy testimonies are my meditation.*
>
> PSALM 119:99

The Word of God will give us understanding. If we meditate on the Word day and night, it will make our way prosperous—then we will have good success (Josh. 1:8). Although we as Christians tend to value a lot of unimportant things above the Word, God still loves us. But if we want to live victorious lives and if we want understanding, we have to meditate on the Word.

8a.   Read Psalm 119:9. How do you get from where you are to where you should be?
      By putting God's Word in your heart

8b.   Discussion question: Why does the Word of God need to be in your heart?
      Discussion question

8c.   Read Joshua 1:8. If you want to live a victorious life and if you want understanding, you have to _____ on the Word.
      Meditate

9. God directs your steps, but He doesn't show you the end of the path from the very beginning (Ps. 119:105), because He loves you. When God Almighty takes the time to talk to you and tell you to do something, why would you try to reason it all out in order to decide whether you're going to do it or not? If that's the way you think, you aren't absolutely convinced that God is working for your best interest. I would rather step out in what I think God is telling me to do and be wrong than not do what He is telling me to because I want to play it safe. God knows what He is doing and the challenges you will face. I don't want any of the miracles that God has put on the inside of me still there when I leave this world; I want to get them all out—I want to go for it! As you read God's Word, He will tell you something and then you act on it. After you step into what God has said, you will be able to see the next step, and the next step, and so on.

9a. Read Psalm 119:105. God directs your steps, but why doesn't He show you the end of the path from the very beginning?
Because He loves you

9b. If God tells you to do something and you try to reason it all out in order to decide whether you're going to do it or not, what aren't you absolutely convinced of?
A. That you won't have another chance
B. What you will do instead of what God has said
C. That God is working for your best interest
D. All of the above
E. None of the above
C. That God is working for your best interest

9c. True or false: After you step into what God has said, you will be able to see the next step, and the next step, and so on.
True

10. Seeds don't immediately sprout into fruit-bearing plants (Mark 4:26-29). It's a process: first the blade, then the ear of corn buds, and later the full fruit of corn appears. The will of God comes in the same way: step by step. Understanding this principle will really help you. There is a growth process involved in finding, following, and fulfilling God's will for your life. After you have been following God's leading for a while, maybe you will begin to see a bigger picture—but you won't get it all at once.

10a. Read Mark 4:26-29. Understanding what principle will really help you?
That the will of God comes step by step

10b. What is involved in finding, following, and fulfilling God's will for your life?
A. Making friends
B. Having enough money saved up
C. Getting man's approval
D. Plenty of sunlight
E. A growth process
E. A growth process

11. The strength of a person lies in his or her focus (Phil. 3:13-14). Paul said *"this* one *thing I do"* (emphasis mine), and that's the reason he turned the world "right-side up." You have to be focused if you want to really accomplish something. The way to kill a person's vision is to give them two visions. Walking in the ways of the world hinders spiritual understanding; therefore, society is not conducive to knowing God. Sadly, a lot of Christians are plugged into the world, and their hearts are divided, their understanding is darkened, and they are alienated from the life of God. *Trying to build a relationship with God on scraps of discarded time is not going to bring you to the center of His will.* You have to make fellowship with God and reading His Word a priority.

11a. Read Philippians 3:13-14. What do you have to be if you want to really accomplish something?
Focused

11b. The way to kill a person's vision is to give them _____ visions.
Two

11c. Discussion question: What do you think it means to be "plugged into the world"?
Discussion question

11d. What won't bring you to the center of God's will?
Trying to build a relationship with God on scraps of discarded time

11e. You have to make fellowship with God _____ reading His Word a priority.
And

12. If you have made some mistakes or have been discouraged or hurt, the Word of God will convert your soul (Ps. 19:7-8)—it will restore your joy and your faith. The soul is the mental and emotional part of you that can experience turmoil—but your born-again spirit is perfect, and the Word will remind you of your true identity. God's Word will make you wise—it will enlighten your eyes. This passage isn't talking about your physical eyes; it's talking about the ability to see with your heart: to see by faith and perceive spiritual things that your physical eyes can't see. The Word of God will open your heart to know things that you can't know by your five senses.

12a. Read Psalm 19:7-8. What will convert your soul—restore your joy and your faith?
A. Your neighbor
B. The Word of God
C. The best new sitcom
D. All of the above
E. None of the above
B. The Word of God

12b. Discussion question: Why do you need to see with your heart: to see by faith and perceive spiritual things?
Discussion question

13. The Word is God is the answer for *any* and *every* problem you might have. The Bible contains God's wisdom for man and everything you need for life and godliness. I believe that the *King James* translation is the best version available, but if you can't handle the "thees" and "thous," then get a translation you enjoy reading. Getting into the Word and learning God's way of thinking is the path to finding His will for your life. Finding God's will for your life will give you a clear purpose and keep you from getting sidetracked by the challenges you face. Knowing that you are doing what God created you to do will give you strength to weather the storms of life.

13a. What contains God's wisdom for man and everything you need for life and godliness?
    A. The internet
    B. Astrology
    C. The Bible
    D. A financial consultant
    E. Children
    C. The Bible

13b. True or false: Knowing that you are doing what God created you to do will give you strength to weather the storms of life.
    True

14. God has never made a piece of junk—He has never made a failure. Every person born into this world was created by God for a special purpose. Being in the center of God's will brings a sense of fulfillment. The relationship you form with God will spill over into your life and bless the people around you. The best part is that God's will isn't hard to find—He wants you to know it! Once you make the commitment to find God's will, you will see Him begin to move in your life, and awesome things will start to happen.

14a. What brings a sense of fulfillment?
    Being in the center of God's will

14b. The relationship who forms with God will spill over into their life and bless the people around them?
    You

14c. True or false: The best part is that God's will is hard to find.
    False

14d. Discussion question: Why is a commitment to finding God's will needed before you see Him begin to move in your life?
    Discussion question

DISCIPLESHIP QUESTIONS • 5.2

23. Read Psalm 119:9. How do you get from where you are to where you should be?

_____

_____

_____

24. Discussion question: Why does the Word of God need to be in your heart?

_____

_____

_____

25. Read Joshua 1:8. If you want to live a victorious life and if you want understanding, you have to _____ on the Word.

26. Read Psalm 119:105. God directs your steps, but why doesn't He show you the end of the path from the very beginning?

_____

_____

_____

27. If God tells you to do something and you try to reason it all out in order to decide whether you're going to do it or not, what aren't you absolutely convinced of?
   A. That you won't have another chance
   B. What you will do instead of what God has said
   C. That God is working for your best interest
   D. All of the above
   E. None of the above

28. True or false: After you step into what God has said, you will be able to see the next step, and the next step, and so on.

29. Read Mark 4:26-29. Understanding what principle will really help you?

_____

_____

_____

30. What is involved in finding, following, and fulfilling God's will for your life?
    A. Making friends
    B. Having enough money saved up
    C. Getting man's approval
    D. Plenty of sunlight
    E. A growth process

31. Read Philippians 3:13-14. What do you have to be if you want to really accomplish something?

    _____

    _____

    _____

32. The way to kill a person's vision is to give them _____ visions.

33. Discussion question: What do you think it means to be "plugged into the world"?

    _____

    _____

    _____

34. What won't bring you to the center of God's will?

    _____

    _____

    _____

35. You have to make fellowship with God _____ reading His Word a priority.

36. Read Psalm 19:7-8. What will convert your soul—restore your joy and your faith?
    A. Your neighbor
    B. The Word of God
    C. The best new sitcom
    D. All of the above
    E. None of the above

37. Discussion question: Why do you need to see with your heart: to see by faith and perceive spiritual things?

_____

_____

_____

38. What contains God's wisdom for man and everything you need for life and godliness?
    A. The internet
    B. Astrology
    C. The Bible
    D. A financial consultant
    E. Children

39. True or false: Knowing that you are doing what God created you to do will give you strength to weather the storms of life.

40. What brings a sense of fulfillment?

_____

_____

_____

41. The relationship who forms with God will spill over into their life and bless the people around them?

_____

_____

_____

42. True or false: The best part is that God's will is hard to find.

43. Discussion question: Why is a commitment to finding God's will needed before you see Him begin to move in your life?

_____

_____

_____

23. By putting God's Word in your heart
24. *Discussion question*
25. Meditate
26. Because He loves you
27. C. That God is working for your best interest
28. True
29. That the will of God comes step by step
30. E. A growth process
31. Focused
32. Two
33. *Discussion question*
34. Trying to build a relationship with God on scraps of discarded time
35. And
36. B. The Word of God
37. *Discussion question*
38. C. The Bible
39. True
40. Being in the center of God's will
41. You
42. False
43. *Discussion question*

PSALM 119:9

Wherewithal shall a young man cleanse his way? by taking heed thereto according to thy word.

PSALM 119:99

I have more understanding than all my teachers: for thy testimonies are my meditation.

JOSHUA 1:8

This book of the law shall not depart out of thy mouth; but thou shalt meditate therein day and night, that thou mayest observe to do according to all that is written therein: for then thou shalt make thy way prosperous, and then thou shalt have good success.

PSALM 119:105

Thy word is a lamp unto my feet, and a light unto my path.

MARK 4:26-29

And he said, So is the kingdom of God, as if a man should cast seed into the ground; [27] And should sleep, and rise night and day, and the seed should spring and grow up, he knoweth not how. [28] For the earth bringeth forth fruit of herself; first the blade, then the ear, after that the full corn in the ear. [29] But when the fruit is brought forth, immediately he putteth in the sickle, because the harvest is come.

PHILIPPIANS 3:13-14

Brethren, I count not myself to have apprehended: but this one thing I do, forgetting those things which are behind, and reaching forth unto those things which are before, [14] I press toward the mark for the prize of the high calling of God in Christ Jesus.

PSALM 19:7-8

The law of the LORD is perfect, converting the soul: the testimony of the LORD is sure, making wise the simple. [8] The statutes of the LORD are right, rejoicing the heart: the commandment of the LORD is pure, enlightening the eyes.

LESSON 5.1
Spirit, Soul & Body

This teaching is a foundational truth that is essential for understanding how much God loves you and believing what He says about you in His Word. Each person is made up of three different parts: spirit, soul, and body. Learn how these three parts relate to God and to each other. At salvation your spirit is totally changed, but your soul and body is not yet redeemed. This series will teach you how to release the life that is already in your spirit, into your physical body and emotions.

Item Code: 1027-C   4-CD album
Item Code: 1027-D   As-Seen-on-TV DVD album
Item Code: 318   Paperback
Item Code: 418   Study Guide

OTHER RECOMMENDED TEACHINGS

Christian Survival Kit
Jesus knew His disciples would face the most trying time of their lives when He went to the cross. So, He gave them vital survival instructions that apply to your life today!

Item Code: 1001-C   16-CD album

Discover the Keys to Staying Full of God
Staying full of God is not a secret or a mystery; it's simple. For that reason, few people recognize the keys, and even fewer practice them. Learn what they are, and put them into practice. They will keep your heart sensitive.

Item Code: 1029-C   4-CD album
Item Code: 1029-D   As-Seen-on-TV DVD album
Item Code: 324   Paperback
Item Code: 424   Study Guide

Don't Limit God X 10
You are the one who determines who God is and what He can do in your life. He is waiting on you. If you doubt that now, you won't after listening to this message.

Item Code: 1076-C   5-CD album
Item Code: 1076-D   As-Seen-on-TV DVD album
Item Code: 3219-D   Recorded Live DVD album

Effortless Change
We all have areas in our lives we want to change. Trying to change from the outside in is difficult. Inside out is effortless. Learn why.

Item Code: 1018-C   4-CD album
Item Code: 1018-D   As-Seen-on-TV DVD album
Item Code: 331   Paperback
Item Code: 431   Study Guide

God's Man, Plan, and Timing
Moses was God's man, and he knew God's plan, but he didn't have a clue as to the timing or how to see the plan come to pass. This message from Andrew will reveal truths from the Moses' life that will ensure you don't make the same mistakes!

Item Code: U05-C   Single CD

OTHER RECOMMENDED TEACHINGS

Hardness of Heart
You might be surprised to find out that all Christians have a degree of hardness in their hearts. Listen as Andrew establishes from Scripture the cause and the cure.

Item Code: 1003-C   4-CD album
Item Code: 1003-D   As-Seen-on-TV DVD album
Item Code: 303   Paperback

Lessons from Elijah
You don't have to experience everything to learn life's lessons. Elijah, a man mightily used of God, is a great example. You'll be blessed from these life examples.

Item Code: 1026-C   5-CD album
Item Code: 1026-D   As-Seen-on-TV DVD album

The Power of Hope
Imagination dictates how your life goes, and if you're ever going to receive what God has for you, you'll need to understand that hope is a *positive* imagination. Learn this and you'll know the true power of hope!

Item Code: 1080-C   5-CD album
Item Code: 1080-D   As-Seen-on-TV DVD album
Item Code: 3221-D   Recorded Live DVD album